Seven Bells
to Bethlehem

The O Antiphons of Advent

Oliver Treanor

First Published in 1995
Gracewing
Fowler Wright Books
Southern Avenue, Leominster
Herefordshire HR6 0QF

Gracewing Books are distributed

In New Zealand by
Catholic Supplies Ltd
80 Adelaide Road
Wellington
New Zealand

In Canada by
Meakin and Associates
Unit 17, 81 Auriga Drive
Nepean, Ontario, KZE 7Y5
Canada

In U.S.A. by
Morehouse Publishing
P.O. Box 1321
Harrisburg
PA 17105
U.S.A.

In Australia by
Charles Paine Pty
8 Ferris Street
North Parramatta
NSW 2151 Australia

ISBN 0 85244 329 3

Typesetting by Action Typesetting Limited, Gloucester
Printed by Cromwell Press, Broughton Gifford, Melksham, Wiltshire,
SN12 8PH

Contents

Abbreviations

GNB   Good News Bible
GS   Past. Const. *Gaudium et spes*
JB   Jerusalem Bible
KNOX   Knox Translation of the Bible
LG   Dogm. Const. *Lumen gentium*
(N)RSV   (New) Revised Standard Version of the Bible
TEV   Today's English Version of the Bible

*   *   *

All scripture citations are taken from the RSV, or NRSV translations of the Bible, unless otherwise stated; except for the Psalms, which are from the *The Grail Version* (as used in the Divine Office).

Foreword

Medieval travellers, they say,
Though worldly-wise, were prone to lose their way
When dark December's darkest evenings fell.
But passing by the Abbey La Fontaine
They found their way again,
Remembering Emmanuel.

Their journey broken by a seven-night rest, to them
Was brought a new direction as to men of old
To whom, the Gospel says, God's wisdom did belong.
For as the monks were singing Mary's Song
The expectant church, as was her wont, tolled
Seven bells to Bethlehem.

It was the custom in the Middle Ages throughout the monasteries of Europe to sing the O antiphons with the Magnificat at Vespers in the week leading up to Christmas. Each evening from December 17 to 23, the antiphon proper to the Office was intoned by a different monk in descending rank order, beginning with the Abbot.

During the singing of the Canticle and its antiphon the largest bell in the community was rung from the campanile. Like the Angelus bell today which calls to mind the incarnation, it called the faithful to rejoice as it marked off the days approaching the Nativity. Wherever its sonorous tone was heard – over high slopes in Germany or France, along upper Alpine valleys, across Swiss mountain cantons or down on the flood plains of Italy – it invited men to join with the spirit of Mary on her journey to Bethlehem, and to share with her, through repentance and prayer, the grace of giving birth to the Saviour.

Though far from Palestine, the sound of the seven bells brought Bethlehem close to the hearts and minds of Christians everywhere, but to none more than those who chanted the antiphons and pondered deeply on their meaning.

Introduction:
The Great 'O' of Advent

From the eighth century they have been chanted by the people of God at Vespers in the week leading up to Christmas: the 'O' antiphons of Advent. Among the most beautiful prayers of their kind ever composed, they were the best and final flowering in a season of exceptional antiphonal creativity that began with St Ambrose in the fourth century and lasted nearly 500 years. Nothing ever written in that genre could touch them for sheer excellence of thought and expression, not even the so-called Marian antiphons of the fourteenth century (which are more properly hymns).

The 'O' antiphons are the distinctive prayers of Advent. They hallow the time of preparation for Christ's birth. That this is the case is partly because they belong to the liturgy — the Divine Office which sanctifies the Hours, and the Eucharist which centres and completes the consecration of the day to the Lord, and partly because they are themselves a rich source of meditation on Advent and on the One whose coming is ardently awaited.

Through the seven days before Christmas Eve they are recited before and after the Magnificat, and as the versicle which precedes the gospel at Mass. Thrice daily from December 17th, like bells tolling the hours of winter daylight and darkness as the Nativity draws near. The three and the seven — numbers denoting completeness in the sacred numerology of Judeo-Christian tradition. The period of waiting, they seem to say, is nearly over. The cycle of time is almost complete: like the closing of a perfect circle.

1

The very shape of the 'O' which gives them their name conveys this. It is a figure of fullness. A kind of hieroglyph of that text in St Paul which puts into words what the symbolic 'O' signifies. 'When the time had fully come, God sent forth his Son, born of a woman ... so that we might receive adoption as sons' (Gal. 4:4−5). The yearly round of Advent recalls the perfection of God's timing in the mystery of redemption. It makes that moment present again through thankful remembrance. But more than this, it proclaims that Time itself is fulfilled, being now filled with the fullness of him in whom dwells the fullness of God. The *pleroma* that St Paul attributed to Christ, that fullness of the divine nature in him who became man, overflows into every age for its sanctification through the reality of his coming. Consequently the completed circle that the antiphons announce is not something static. It is a spiralling maelstrom of love that draws to its inner self all mankind, all history, the very cosmos itself.

Because of this, Advent is not only the celebration of God's coming to us, but also of our coming to him. It is, after all, a season of repentance. So the hour is ripe in a double sense. It is time again to mend the broken circles of our lives by returning, as a circle does, to our point of origin. Christmas makes this possible, for by the birth of God-made-man, man comes back to God in the same moment as he comes to us. Mary's *Fiat* made it so, when she gave all humanity to God in the very act of giving God a humanity.

Since the Great 'O' suggests ripe fullness, it images the womb of the Virgin in late pregnancy, round and full of Christ. From the period when the 'O' antiphons were first sung in the monasteries of Europe, Mary was known as the 'O' Madonna. Medieval frescoes depict the Virgin of Advent large and maternal, venerable through Christ-bearing. The 'O' also reflects the catholicity of the Church, full of the grace of Christ's indwelling in ministry, sacrament, holy scripture and two thousand years of worship. Mary's other title in the Middle Ages was Mother of the Church. Contemporary painting showed her as Mater Ecclesiae sheltering the children of God in her all-encompassing mantle. Thus up to the fourteenth century, art and the antiphons envisaged

Mary and the Church as typified equally by the 'O', sharing the same function that the 'O' represented, of carrying Christ to the world.

To understand Mary was to understand the Church. To honour Mary was to love the Church. The twelfth century Cistercian, Blessed Isaac of Stella, regarded them as synonymous. 'When mention is made of either in the divinely inspired scriptures', he wrote, 'it is to be understood almost indifferently and conjointly of both' (Sermon 51). Never was that conjunction more luminous than in the medieval celebration of Advent, where music and art, liturgy and theology were combined in one profound act of sound and light to render thanks for the incarnation of God and the deification of man.

The Great 'O' then ultimately stands for Mary and the Universal Church, the Virgin pregnant and the Una Sancta Ecclesia: both expectant of the Messiah. One as Mother of the historical Jesus, Head of the Body; the other as Community of eschatological hope in which are born the members of that Body. Each heavy with salvation. Each announcing with perfect conviction the certainty of his coming. As once Mary's enlarged form encircled his first arrival in the flesh, making his epiphany inevitable, so the Christian life, swollen with grace, affirms the inevitability of his second coming in glory at the end of history. Between these two poles runs the axis of his many comings in mystery through the liturgy. Here past and future converge as Eternity enters into time mystically, touching and transforming every present moment into salvation history. Thus the perplexing paradox of faith is rendered eminently meaningful: how Christ can be already come, even as he is still awaited.

From this it is clear that a tension remains between what has already been achieved of our redemption and what has yet to be accomplished, a tension that holds in place the mystery of salvation. Even as we celebrate the triumph of Christ's first coming at Bethlehem we are preparing ourselves for his ultimate victory at the eschaton. The Advent antiphons express this tension in the way they are constructed. Each consists of an invocation followed by an acclamation and then a supplication. In these three ways they affirm that the Messiah has already come *and* that he has yet to appear. Thus they endorse the message of Advent itself. In fact, because they have been sung for so many centuries they assert that the whole Christian era, from Pentecost to Parousia, is one continuous Advent, the age of joyful suspense, the age of the Spirit and of the Church.

The invocations call on the Child of Mary's womb with names that are full of faith. As Mary herself undoubtedly did in those last few days of tender contemplation before his birth. O Wisdom! O Adonai! O Root of Jesse! O Key of David! O Rising Sun! O Desire of Nations! O Emmanuel! Here is a Child that is deeply desired: on him rests the fate of a people broken by sin, a people as good as dead until brought to second birth. Thus the capital 'O' is first of all a vocative 'O'. It addresses each title to the Messiah personally, though he be invisible. Invisible, but not absent. While hidden in the depths of his Mother, he is as present as in the baptized soul of every Christian. His glory too is there. Though eclipsed by his infancy, it is as real as its own reflection in the womb of every heart that longs for him. Thus the tension is maintained and respected: weak he may be in his nameless embryonic state, but by his titles of honour he brings a power that will save.

This is why the 'O' is repeated at the end of the antiphon – this time as an urgent supplication. 'O come and teach us', 'O come and save', 'O come to deliver us', 'O come to free the captive', 'O come and enlighten us', 'O come and save man', 'O come and save us'. We who make these appeals may well be redeemed, but we labour under the shadow of original sin. Until he comes to be fully formed in us, as once he was in Mary, we cannot grow 'to mature manhood, to the measure of the stature of the fulness of Christ' (Eph. 4:13). Each exclamation consequently signifies desperate need and desperate hope. Upon his safe delivery depends our safe deliverance.

The acclamations follow the christological titles. They share the same sublime purpose of the Magnificat: to herald the grandeur of salvation that the Son of God will bring. 'You fill the universe and hold all things together'; 'You appeared to Moses and gave him the law'; 'You stand as an ensign for the nations'; 'What you open no one can close again'; 'You

are the splendour of eternal light and the sun of justice';
'You are the cornerstone which makes all one'; 'You are
our king and judge, the Saviour'.

As it considers the Nativity in the light of these messianic
metaphors – drawn mostly from Isaiah (the Old Testament
precursor of the first coming), and from the Apocalypse
(which anticipates the last) – the Church sees in Mary the
bearer of the Promises, and in Jesus their utter fulfilment.
But in a way that surpasses expectation. His incarnation
challenges our very concept of God, overturns our notion of
his mighty power, topples our delusions of the Ideal Saviour.
At his long-awaited coming he revealed a Deity so small that
he could not even be seen. As tiny as a fertilized ovum. So
insignificant even at birth that the world disregarded him. So
abject at his death that it roundly rejected him. It requires
a voice of praise and proclamation – the voice of Mary
long ago, the voice of the Church ever since – to lift him
up high enough to be noticed and to magnify the hidden
magnificence of his mercy. This is why the antiphons, like
the Magnificat, are the songs of the poor in spirit. Those
at the fringe of things, the unimportant, have always seen
from the periphery what is missed at the core of religiously
indifferent society.

It is fitting that the anthems addressed to the Virgin's Son
should be sung in tune with Mary's own Canticle praising the
Lord's greatness, in which she herself is declared blessed for
all generations. Like garlands round an icon, the 'O' antiphons adorn the Mother while adoring the Son, honour
her virginal poverty along with his wealth of compassion,
acknowledge jointly the simple humility of the hand-maid
and the humble magnanimity of her Lord.

Likewise it is fitting that the antiphons should be incorporated into the Mass. It reinforces the intrinsic relationship
between the Divine Office and the Eucharistic Celebration,
the one leading to the other and extending, through the
Prayer of the Hours, 'the memorial of the mysteries of salvation and the foretaste of heavenly glory, which are offered
us in the eucharistic mystery' (*General Instruction on the Liturgy of the Hours*, §12).

As the prelude to the gospel, the 'O' antiphons perfectly
fulfil, by their very theme and structure, the purpose of the

Alleluiah verse, to 'serve as the assembled faithful's greeting of welcome to the Lord' (*General Introduction to the Roman Missal*, §23). Especially since, from December 17th onward, the gospel readings are taken from the Infancy Narratives of Matthew and Luke. True to the spirit of these readings, they pick up their sense of expectancy and orchestrate their tone of anticipation. Invoking, acclaiming, supplicating, they match the mood of the Word itself, inspiring the congregation to a deeper desire for him who is conceived in the mind before being born in the will.

But their association with the Mass is particularly apposite because of the Eucharist itself. Here is all Advent in Sacrament; his coming, his birth, his death and resurrection, his many comings, his eschatological pledge. Here he is truly present in Person; here he is gently concealed in his most humble form. Here, in full, is all that has already been achieved; here is all that is yet to be accomplished. This is God and Mary's Son, Head of the Body in whom are all the members too. For the monks and mystics of the Middle Ages it was only natural that the 'O Emmanuel!' should precede and lead to the cry, 'O latens Deitas! (O Hidden Godhead)', of thirteenth century eucharistic adoration.

Finally, insofar as the liturgical action of the Mass is the efficacious memorial of the Paschal Mystery, it provides an ideal setting for the Advent antiphons. For they too recall, albeit in anticipation, the New Passover of Jesus, thereby reminding us that Christmas is not celebrated as an end in itself but is oriented towards the Easter festival, climax of the liturgical year. While not sacramentally efficacious as is the Eucharist, the antiphons are nevertheless instruments of grace. They prepare the way for belief by proclaiming, as Advent is meant to do, the Apostolic *kerygma* – the essential Mystery of Faith – whose reality is rendered present in the Eucharist, and whose grace is distributed through the sacramental life of the Church.

Chapter 1

The 'O' Madonna

On a visit some years ago to a friend who is a priest in Spain, I was taken to see an unusual statue of Our Lady. Don Jaime is pastor to a scatter of diminishing mountain villages in the northern province of Huesca. In one of these stands a fine, very old stone church and it was here, in the crypt, that he introduced me to La Madona de la O – the 'O' Madonna. It represents the Mother of God in late pregnancy, round and full-blossomed like the capital 'O', with the fullness of Christ. Under this title she is venerated locally as one who, full of grace, carries within her the very source of Life and our hope of resurrection. Heavy with the devotional weight of centuries, the image miraculously survived the ravages of the Spanish Civil War. It was transferred at that time to the safety of the crypt by the fathers of the present parishioners because of its great significance for them. There the Virgin still encloses in the crypt of her womb the secret centre of history, the key to human destiny, in the face of the most appalling suffering imaginable: the warfare, poverty and depopulation of the twentieth century. By her largesse she quietly announces the divine empathy that dwells in our midst. To all who contemplate the statue there comes a sense of serene and thrilling expectancy, of something about to happen. Though invisible, Christ is truly present within Mary. Though not yet born he is already tangibly here. As I studied this ancient work of art it occurred to me that it also represented the Church in Advent.

Like the Virgin Mother, the Church proclaims the certainty of Christ's coming. It is not a matter of maybe or might. It is an assured certainty, like that of one about to give birth. In its preaching there is an urgency born of confidence as it prepares God's people for his final appearing at the end of time when he will deal his decisive blow on evil. Then he will create a new heaven and a new earth as he promised, the perfect setting for his reign of justice and peace which will last forever. We look forward to this victory daily as we pray, 'Thy kingdom come!'; but in Advent we focus our faith more finely, anticipating this arrival with all the emotions of an expectant mother. 'We wait in joyful hope for the coming of our Saviour, Jesus Christ', is how the liturgy puts it. On that day our welcome will be as strong and true as Mary's was when she laid him in the manger at Bethlehem. At his second appearance with his angel hosts of power, we shall gaze on his face with an ecstasy long desired, as his Mother did before us in the presence of his angels at the crib.

Yet between that first coming in the flesh at Christmas and his second coming in glory at the end of history, Christ is constantly living and growing in the Church, as the 'O' Madonna reminds us. Through grace he is increasing like the unborn child in the womb of every soul that longs for him. We can feel his presence in prayer as Mary felt him in the last month of her confinement. She listened at night for his heart-beat, rejoiced when she felt him kick, relaxed when he settled to rest. In an analogous way spiritually, he moves gently in the silence of the attentive heart of the Christian. Without any need for words, he lets us know he is there. As we guard that Life within us until its ultimate appearance at our life's end, we pray that even now through the on-going Advent of contemplation, right choices and graced action, we may bring him to maturity within us mystically, that we may give him safe delivery.

This was Paul's wish for his churches in Galatia. 'My little children', he wrote them, 'I am in travail until Christ be formed in you!' (Gal. 4:19). It is still the Church's wish today. That the Word might become flesh in our flesh by holiness of life. That together the community of believers might make visible the Body of Christ by deeper participation in the sacramental life, by their acts of public worship, by praying the Liturgy of the Hours, and above all by celebrating the Eucharist with wonder and awe. Mary in Advent is especially vigilant over those who carry her Son through the modern world. As our Mother the Church she intercedes for her children with the Holy Spirit lest Christ be still-born through the stubbornness of unrepented sin. For there is no sadness so great as the loss of one's child, particularly when that Child is the Lord.

Without doubt in the last few days before Jesus' birth his Mother spoke to him tenderly, called him forth with affectionate names that only a mother knows. The Church imitates her example. In the seven days before Christmas Eve at Evening Prayer, Mary's Magnificat − her song of pregnant joy − is prefaced by what we call the 'O' antiphons, short versicles that also form the Alleluiah verse before the gospel at the Mass of that day. They invoke the Christ Child with titles of reverence and praise as we mark off the time to Nativity. They encapsulate the faith of the season, arouse our desire for his coming, make us reflect on the meaning of his identity. They express the fact that he is a child that is wanted, that his birth alone can pacify the profound longing of the human race. 'Come, O Wisdom! O Adonai! Come, O Stock of Jesse! O Key of David, come! O Rising Sun! O Desire of Nations, come! O come, O come, Emmanuel!'

Forming a long tradition in the Western Church that goes back to the eighth century, these acclamations are drawn from a wide span of Old Testament scripture including its Wisdom literature, the Law and prophecy. The titles come mostly from Isaiah, the prophet *par excellence* of the messianic promises and therefore himself a classic Advent figure. Like Mary, John the Baptist and St Paul in different times, he pointed the attention of the people to the One who was to come. Frequently he did so in images that were covert, not immediately comprehensible. His often mysterious prefigurements and types of the Deliverer were designed to stimulate Israel's understanding of God's purposes as well as their hopes and expectations. Indeed, like Jesus' parables, his metaphorical passages were meant to distinguish those who were open to the Word and sincerely sought its meaning from those who were not. The messianic allusions of this poet-prophet would mean little or nothing to the group whose hearts were 'fat, and their ears heavy'

and who 'shut their eyes', who would 'hear and hear but
not understand, see and see but not perceive' (6:10, 9). But
the Christian Church at prayer is not composed of such as
these. Taking up the Advent antiphons again year by year,
it savours continually the significance of the ancient titles
of promise, creating a reverberating mantra of consistent
gratitude down the Christian centuries.

To the Israelites who did heed Isaiah's message, the messianic prophecies were a source of immense comfort and
consolation. In times of political and spiritual trauma, Isaiah
was a true apostle to the nation in distress. He knew the
condition of his people. He recognized their need for deliverance. Hence he left them − and us − with more portraits
of the Saviour than any other writer of the Old Testament,
lightening the very darkest moments with the bright hope of
his coming. Which is why undoubtedly his prophetic titles
were seized upon by the writer of the Apocalypse where they
abound. Written late in the first century AD to encourage
the young churches under severe persecution, the final book
of the Bible addresses a situation not unlike that in which
Isaiah wrote. Adapting their relevance to the particular circumstances of each community, the author reveals their
salvific fulfilment in Jesus himself. However they are still
used as pointers to a future eschatological event. Whereas in
the Old Testament they foretold the Messiah's first coming,
now they predict his second. Penned at a time when the
primitive churches were adjusting their expectations of an
immanent Parousia, contenting themselves that the end was
not so soon, the Apocalypse found inspiration in the Hebrew
types for calling the baptized to a new readiness for Jesus
whenever he would choose to appear.

The titles enshrined in the 'O' antiphons are therefore
distinctively New Testament in character even though their
origins lie in the Jewish tradition. In this sense they unite
both the old and the new dispensations through the common
hope of God's chosen people. Jews and Gentiles alike, we
await the complete unfolding of the Lord's plan to save his
children. Advent reminds us that we are a people of promise
and that as such we shall not be disappointed. God does not
revoke his promises (Rom. 11:29; 5:5). As Christians our
hope is doubly strong. We believe that in Christ all God's

promises are already in place. His first coming at the incarnation confirmed the reliability of the prophetic word. The enduring presence of his Spirit in the Church, by which the final age has already dawned, assures us that he will return again. In a real way the future has begun in the here and now. What we expect will not be unlike what we are presently experiencing (1 John 3:2). The Church's expectancy is not for something entirely new. It already knows intimately the One it is seeking. He is her brother, her spouse, her son.

The Liturgy of the Hours jubilantly incorporates the Judeo-Christian messianic epithets in its Advent antiphons because they are christological titles. All our worship is centred on Christ, is through Christ and is in Christ. To call on him is to touch God himself; to know him is to know the Father; to pray through his name is to pray in the Spirit. When we invoke him by common acclamation at Evening Prayer in the pre-Nativity octave, we ponder that name and its holiness, believing that 'there is no other name under heaven ... by which we must be saved' (Acts 4:12) since it is 'the name which is above every name,' at which 'every knee should bow, in heaven and on earth and under the earth' (Phil. 2:10). In doing so we echo the polyphonic chorus that concludes the Book of Revelation and the Bible, the last words of God's Word, intoned by the Spirit himself, the bridal Church, the writer of the book, the one who is thirsty, and the reader who hears:

('Behold, I am coming soon').
The Spirit and the Bride say, 'Come'. And let him who hears say, 'Come'. And let him who is thirsty come.
('Surely I am coming soon').
Amen. So be it.
Maranatha, Come, Lord Jesus!

Past, present and future converge in the liturgy. The eternal enters into time. Through the sanctification of the Hours, *chronos* is transformed into *kairos* — the golden opportunity for grace. 'It is full time now for you to wake from sleep. For salvation is nearer to us now than when we first believed; the night is far gone, the day is at hand' (Rom.

13:11–12). 'Behold, now is the acceptable time; behold, now is the day of salvation' (2 Cor. 6:2). It is a moment of intense consciousness of the need to respond before it is too late. The Time is ripe in a dual sense. Not only is this the Church's Advent. It is Advent in heaven too. God is waiting for our coming to him just as we wait for his coming to us. At baptism he celebrated our first re-birth. At death he anticipates our second. In the interim he watches out, like the Father of the prodigal son, for our many returns to him through conversion and repentance.

The vocative-O of the antiphons combines both perspectives on Advent. It articulates our wish that once again what St Paul said in Galatians will come true: 'When the time had fully come, God sent his Son, born of a woman ... so that we might receive adoption as sons' (4:4–5). But the parturition of Christ's Body, which began with the birth of the Head from Mary, is not complete until the deliverance of all his other members too. Deliverance, that is, not only from the embryonic, immature state of being which is the symbol of our spiritual incompleteness, but deliverance also from sin, which is the reality to which the symbol refers. Through the ages the Church, like creation itself, groans in one great act of giving birth. While we know it will continue till the end of time, yet insofar as the labour-pangs are for us, our nativity is now. We cannot therefore truly celebrate Christmas as the birth of the whole Christ, Head and members together, unless our personal development is gaining a roundness and wholeness in the spirit. The shape of the capital 'O' depicts the perfection we mean. As a cry of exclamation to God it also proclaims our belief that our sonship is pure gift and depends upon Christ's coming as Word and as sacrament, as Spirit and as mystery, to bring it to completion.

The context of the antiphons at Vespers is the Magnificat, which they introduce and conclude. A most appropriate setting: Mary's hymn of ecstasy to the Lord who has blessed her name for all generations. The text, reminiscent of similar anthems of praise in the Old Testament including that of Hannah at the conception of Samuel, attributes all greatness and glory to the Almighty. 'My soul glorifies the Lord and my spirit exults in God my Saviour.' The joy of her words rises from a heart overflowing with the Word made flesh. It flies upward to the Father and outward to others, setting the infant in Elizabeth's womb leaping. Like an electric impulse, the voice of the Virgin activates a dynamic parallelogram of sound and motion − from woman to woman, from child to mother, from child to Child − that erupts in a charismatic outpouring of praise and thanks.

It is the spirit of Mary that the worshipping community seeks to re-capture in Advent. The antiphonic acclamations echo her virginal jubilation; the titles articulate the cause of her joy; the repetition of her canticle returns the glory once again back to God; the common recitation of her words re-charges and unites the Church in a single harmony of mind and voice. Like garlands surrounding an icon, the 'O' antiphons highlight the Magnificat as a prayer that perfectly catches the purpose of Advent and rightly deserves special attention in the final phase of this season.

The purpose of Advent is indeed to magnify the Lord in a world that largely overlooks him. It is because the Lord is so small, that is to say unobtrusive in his humility, that he has to be magnified to be seen. Mary's canticle, like the feast of Christmas, challenges our concept of the divine greatness. Contrary to what many expect, his power is made known through weakness, his wisdom through folly. In the 'O' Madonna, God is a child in embryo, a fertilized ovum too tiny in the initial stage to be regarded by the naked eye. Too insignificant even after nine months to be believed in by the eye of incredulity. It requires the voice of praise and proclamation − whether that of the Virgin Mother or of the Church − to draw to the notice of Israel and the modern world respectively the hidden magnificance of his mercy. His coming is an obscure event, easily missed because usually occurring where least anticipated: among the poor in spirit, the down and out, the non-influential, the emarginated. 'He must increase', to quote the words of the Baptist who, like Mary and St Paul and Isaiah, recognized in the Messiah's self-abasement the world's opportunity for salvation and also the danger of letting that opportunity pass through spiritual unpreparedness.

Today the Magnificat antiphons glorify the greatness of the Lord. They enlarge the holiness of his name, spell out the dimensions of his mercy, sound the depths of his profound love. They put words on the lips of the Precursor-Church to announce that the Kingdom of God is at hand, that the time has come to repent and believe the Good News.

'That he might increase' − but also, 'I must decrease'. Advent implies this other side too. It is not possible to magnify the Lord unless the disciple emulates the Master's humility and makes it his own. Mary's paean is a celebration of lowliness and a testimony to its fruitfulness as a state of life. The surrender of self to the service of the divine will is a force that conquers God. It draws him out of his heaven, commands the fullness of his compassion, compels his utter protection against the enemy, demands from him his eternal faithfulness to 'Abraham and his sons forever' − that is the children of faith. By contrast the proud-hearted are scattered, the high and mighty de-throned, the rich are sent away empty. How he achieves this, what Mary means by this, the 'O' antiphons make explicit by the christological titles and the versicles that elaborate Jesus' redemptive work. Culled from the sources of scripture they reveal that he who comes conquers his foes by turning them into friends, defeats sinners by making them into saints, eliminates apathy and hatred by absorbing such frustrations into his love.

The 'O' antiphons are intoned on the seven days before the vigil of Nativity. Seven is the number of fullness according to Jewish sacred numerology which the Christian Church has adopted. Each antiphon is repeated − before and after the Magnificat. Twice seven is fourteen: the fullness of fullness, the *pleroma* of St Paul, the key to the structure of Jesus' genealogy in Matthew. They toll the Hours of the maturing season therefore not only by their content but by their numerical signification too. What their measured ringing announces however is more than temporal plenitude. It is the fact that in Christ is found the very fullness of God himself whose nature he shares with us. 'The full content of divine nature lives in Christ, in his humanity, and you have been given full life in union with him' (Col. 2:9 − 10. GNB.). Taken together, the antiphons present to us and celebrate a Jesus who, though stripped of his glory and clothed in humility, remains one hundred per cent God while becoming one hundred per cent man. Losing nothing of his divinity he comes showing us that to be divine we need only become fully human.

The structure of each antiphon is in three parts. Acclamation, invocation, supplication. The acclamatory titles confess the faith of the community by acknowledging, Creed-like, the identity of the One they address. The invocation – 'O, Come!' – professes the community's hope that, since he has always revealed himself as The One-Who-Comes, so he will not delay. The plethora of supplicatory verbs – 'Teach us, save us, deliver us; free those, enlighten those; save man, come and save us' – bespeaks the love that seeks to unite our will with the will of God the Redeemer. But the faith, hope and love that underpin the prayers of Advent are sometimes fragile and often weak. And so, for all the beauty of the language, the antiphons are a cry from a wounded people who have known the loss of grace and dignity through sin.

The petitions they contain, therefore, are not composed for aesthetic pleasure or mere literary appreciation. They are carefully planned to articulate the very real need of the whole of mankind, a fallen race which, though redeemed, is not yet fully saved. What they request corresponds to the state of the human condition as revealed in scripture and by the experience of every thinking person. The antiphons are the fruit of the Church's prolonged examination of conscience. Such self-scrutiny is feasible precisely because of Christmas. Advent is there to encourage and assure God's people that, when we admit our insufficiency, God comes. As the First Letter of John has it, 'If we say we have no sin, we deceive ourselves, and the truth is not in us. If we confess our sins, he is faithful and just, and will forgive our sins and cleanse us from all unrighteousness ... If anyone does sin, we have an advocate with the Father, Jesus Christ the righteous; and he is the expiation for our sins, and not for ours only but also for the sins of the whole world' (1:8−9; 2:1−2).

It is the Church's confidence in these gracious words that makes the owning of sin, implied in the Magnificat versicles, such a joyful and not pessimistic experience. It has grasped as Good News what God is telling it through the liturgies of Advent and Christmas-tide: that sin, once admitted, is no obstacle to his love, since it is for sinners that the Son of God became Son of Man, to transform the sons of men into sons of God.

Hence it is with joyful sorrow, self-deprecating dignity, and humble pride that Christians pronounce the two-fold truth about God and man through the spiritual treasure of the 'O' antiphons in the week before Christmas:

- What was lost by Adam's folly, the Wisdom of Jesus restores by his becoming man;
- What grace was prefigured on Sinai in the Law, Jesus bestows as Lord by the gift of his Pentecost Spirit;
- What died when Jesse's tree was cut to the root, Jesus, its new shoot, revitalizes by his crucifixion;
- What sin slammed shut in Paradise, Jesus, Key of David, re-opens by his ascension into glory;
- What deliverance from death Prophecy dreamt of at its setting, the Jesus of Easter accomplishes as the Rising Sun at his resurrection;
- What Israel in exile foreshadowed, Jesus, Desire of Nations, completes by drawing all things to himself; and
- What God's forsaken people of the Old Dispensation longed for most, Jesus Emmanuel satisfies by his enduring presence as God-with-us.

Chapter Two

O Wisdom

December 17th. O Wisdom, you come forth from the mouth of the Most High.
You fill the universe and hold all things together in a strong yet gentle manner. O come to teach us the way of truth.

When St Paul prayed for the young Christian communities of Asia Minor and Greece his intention was always very specific. The petition attributed to him for the Church at Colossae is one such example: 'We ask God to fill you with the knowledge of his will, with all the wisdom and understanding that his Spirit gives. Then you will be able to live as the Lord wants, and always do what pleases him. Your lives will be fruitful in all kinds of good works, and you will grow in your knowledge of God. May you be made strong with all the strength which comes from his glorious might, so that you may be able to endure everything with patience' (Col. 1:9–11. TEV).

To live as God wills is to have wisdom. It requires knowledge and understanding. It brings inner strength and fruitfulness. All these are gifts of the Holy Spirit and are signs of his presence within the Christian. Today the Church makes this its first petition at the intercessions of the first Vespers of Advent. 'You will bring us wisdom, fresh understanding and new vision – Come, Lord Jesus, do not delay!' It is repeated on the third Sunday of the season, and again on the Feast of the Presentation, forty days after Christmas. The recurrence of the plea for wisdom, together with the great supplication for this gift of gifts in the 'O' antiphon on December 17th, leaves no doubt

17

about its primacy in the Church's list of priorities. Like St
Paul we have come to see that without God's wisdom we
cannot please the Lord, cannot house the Spirit within us,
cannot know Christ. How appropriate then that in Advent
as we ponder the meaning of the Lord's coming we should
begin by asking for that which it pleased God to bestow on
Solomon because he desired it above all other things.

Solomon, St Paul, the Church — spanning the length
and breadth of salvation history — cry out to heaven
for something that is staff of life to mankind's spiritual
appetite. How to live wisely, with integrity, uprightly, with
the goodness that brings self-respect. How to achieve a
meaningful human existence through noble character and
conduct, free from the tyranny of egotism and its retinue —
fear, insecurity, suspicion, alienation and despair.

The entire Old Testament is a search for the answer to
this question. It is no exaggeration to say that the Hebrew
hunger for wisdom became a holy obsession with them.
A whole segment of their scripture was devoted to the
practical pursuit of high-principled living. They cherished
a myriad of skilful proverbs and wise maxims that enshrined
certain standards of decency and morality distilled from
their experience of the world and its ways. Not only their
so-called Wisdom literature, but the Mosaic Law too, was
centred on this ideal. By the time of Jesus the virtue of the
Decalogue had so sapped through Jewish society that its
branches were heavy with more than six hundred prescripts
for determining the right thing to do in as many situations.
Their sacred mythology explored the need for such wisdom
by examining the wretchedness of the human condition when
left to its own devices. Sifting through the popular allegories
of Middle Eastern folk-lore, borrowing fables from their
Mesopotamian neighbours, adapting, editing, re-working
ancient oral and written traditions, they compiled a distinctive response to the problem of sin that eventually
became the foundation for Christian thought and doctrine.
Upon one conclusion all the biblical genres concur directly or
indirectly: nothing but God's wisdom can salvage the ignorance of the human race. 'For even if one is perfect among
the sons of men', to quote the venerable scribe who put the
point so prayerfully in his beautiful Canticle of Wisdom, 'yet

without the wisdom that comes from You, O God, he will be regarded as nothing' (Wis. 6:9).

The original fault that breached the dyke of sin and death was Adam's want of understanding. The Genesis account makes it clear that he and his wife were deceived. Ironically he was tempted by the tree of knowledge. Had he possessed wisdom he would not have dared meddle with the dark side of reason. His disobedience was caused by pride. 'You will not die', the serpent had lied to Eve, 'For God knows that when you eat of it your eyes will be opened, and you will be like God' (3:4–5). To be God-like is the reason men seek wisdom. However, to attempt to steal wisdom by gorging on knowledge indiscriminately while deliberately ignoring God's word, is to become Satanic. Interestingly, the wise and learned Priestly editor of the sixth century BC, who shrewdly placed this composition at the beginning of the Bible as a primary lesson in Jewish catechesis, clearly recognized what his mythological forefather did not: that worldly wisdom is a perverse distortion of Truth, which is the property of God alone.

This is precisely the point made by Paul in his Corinthian correspondence. 'Since, in the wisdom of God, the world did not know God through wisdom, it pleased God through the folly of what we preach to save those who believe' (1 Cor. 1:21). What Paul preached was Christ crucified, folly indeed to the philosophical arrogance of the Greeks and a stumbling block to the scandalized Jews. But for those who did accept the gospel, here was 'the power of God and the wisdom of God ... Christ Jesus whom God made our wisdom, our righteousness and sanctification and redemption' (1:24; 30).

This is why the Advent Church cries out, 'O come to teach us the way of truth'. With St Paul and the authors of Genesis it perceives how dangerously reality is disfigured by proud disobedience in the cracked mirror of sinful nature. Without Christ, what is actually detrimental appears worthy and desirable. In him, what seems foolish is far from so. 'For the foolishness of God is wiser than men, and the weakness of God is stronger than men' (1 Cor. 1:25). Therefore it looks out eagerly for the One who comes because he is the new Adam. Replaying the age-old scenario, he stretched out

his hand to a tree 'not counting equality with God a thing
to be grasped' (Phil. 2:6), but humbling himself obediently
unto death, in this way plucking the fruit of wisdom for his
wife the Church to eat, and making his cross the tree of Life.
It stands in the centre of Paradise — not the idyllic Eden of
ignorance and immaturity, but the kingdom of adult innocence that is won by all who grow up in Christ to the
sanctifying knowledge and understanding of the gospel.   ·

The gospel and the cross are one. Calvary is a dramati-
zation of the message contained in the good news. What
Jesus preached in words he acted out in the dread mime
of his passion. So fearful was the play that even his disciples ran away. What they had failed to grasp in his speech
they could not fail to understand in his Golgotha. Words
and actions together in Jesus so completely contradicted
Adam in Eden that the whole world thought Jesus completely mad. When he instructed them to love their enemy
and turn the other cheek they did not believe him until he
meekly accepted the abuse of Pilate's militia and prayed
for those who nailed him to the tree. When he set forth
children as models of the citizens of heaven, said that the
greatest among them would be those who serve, they could
not imagine such a thing until they witnessed his child-like
simplicity as God's suffering servant on the *via dolorosa*.
The kingship he boasted wore thorns for a crown, bore
a reed for its sceptre, endured a robe of mockery for its
purple, was enthroned on a gibbet. His royal motto — 'He
who loses his life will save it' — made no sense until they
watched his body thrown into the bowels of the earth, and
then encountered the resurrection.

Christ's life and teaching proved the absurdity of Adam's
wisdom by turning human logic on its head. His Gethsemane
of obedience to the Father's will countered the disobedience
of Eden which the first man and his wife passed on to their
progeny. His voluntary investiture with sweat and thorns
— the fate of fallen man and earth — reversed the curse
incurred by human foolishness. His impassive acceptance
of the soldiers' blows corrected the deformity of the sons
of men, originally formed in the image of God. Only with
deep reflection in the light of an Easter community does the
unveiling of the mystery of the cross illuminate the paradox

of Jesus: that to be mature you have to become as children are, to be great you must become small, to be first you must be last of all, to live you must die, to be wise you must embrace foolishness.

That this should make no sense to the modern world is not a surprise. Why should an intelligent race that prides itself on technological progress believe what is contrary to its senses? Why should individuals, nourished as we are on the principle of achievement, productivity, control, competition and success, suddenly reverse gear and settle for a system indifferent to such goals, one based on love of God and neighbour? To be modern is to harness love as we have harnessed the other elements of nature. It is to rationalize Religion − bring it into line with the streamlined Objective − and to socialize duty to neighbour in a sensible manner that respects the limits of budget and does not encroach on the democratic idol of enabling those who can afford it to get exactly what they want.

To intone the great 'O Wisdom' of the antiphon is to stand against Efficiency and Success. It is to recognize that idolatry does not change, only its forms. It is to acknowledge the absurdity of contemporary wisdom − the depersonalization of the Unborn; the degradation of human dignity through genetic engineering; the despoliation of relationships by laboratory parenting; the human sacrifice of the unemployed to the demigod, Economy; the inadequate concern for the poor and the homeless, the elderly and the ill. It is to acknowledge also the blindness of a society which, after approving such absurdity, then queries naively the rising crime rate, increased incidence of suicide, disaffection of its citizens and widespread collapse of family life.

The moral world of Jesus' time was not so different from our own. Human nature does not change. Jesus understood that nature very well. As John's Gospel wryly remarks: 'Jesus knew all men and needed no one to bear witness of man; for he himself knew what was in man' (2:25). Which is why his teaching made such a profound impression on the crowds who heard him. After the Sermon on the Mount for example: 'The crowds were astonished at his teaching, for he taught them as one who had authority, and not as their scribes' (Matt. 7:28–29). And when he returned to Nazareth, his home town, and addressed his own people in the synagogue, 'all spoke well of him, and wondered at the gracious words which proceeded out of his mouth' (Luke 4:22), and many exclaimed, 'Where did this man get all this? What is the wisdom given to him? Is not this the carpenter, the son of Mary?' (Mark 6:2–3).

The wisdom of Jesus alerted his audience to the question of his identity. Here was no ordinary man. The enactment of that wisdom in his works and the quality of his life alerted his disciples to his divinity. Jesus was more than just an extraordinary man. After the paschal event when this insight formally came home it became clear to them that, in Christ, God had not deserted the immoral world. In the Fourth Gospel, 'world' is used in two distinct senses: the first to refer to humanity's state of alienation from grace; the second to identify mankind as the object of God's infinite solicitude. 'For God so loved the world that he sent his only Son, that whoever believes in him should not perish but have eternal life. For God sent the Son into the world, not to condemn the world, but that the world might be saved through him' (3:16–17). Jesus, who preached the good news through his wisdom, became himself the good news preached by the apostolic Church. As Pope St Leo the Great puts it, 'Faith gained deeper understanding and by a leap of the mind began to reach out to the Son as the equal of the Father ... The faith of believers was drawn to touch, not with the hand of the flesh but with the understanding of the spirit, the only-begotten Son, the equal of the Father' (Sermon 2). By the end of the first century that conviction reached a maturity of theological expression in the Prologue of the last of the Gospels to be written: 'In the beginning was the Word, and the Word was with God, and the Word was God ... And the Word became flesh and dwelt among us, full of grace and truth' (1 John 1:1; 14). The explanation for the Nazarene's sublime mind and the purpose of his mission had become evident: he was God's saving Wisdom incarnate.

Hebrew scripture had often personified divine wisdom but never intended the reader to take it in a literal sense. It was a poetic metaphor to give visual form to an idea which, though abstract, was very real to those who desired it. Yet at the incarnation this incredible metaphor became reality. Assessing the unique significance of this fact, the Letter to the Hebrews opens with a precise articulation of what happened. 'In many and various ways God spoke of old to our fathers by the prophets; but in these last days he has spoken to us by a Son, whom he appointed the heir of all things, through whom also he created the world' (1:1−2). The passage echoes John's Prologue. 'All things were made through him, and without him was not anything made that was made' (1:3). Both texts had in mind the creation account of Genesis which initiates the story of divine revelation. There it is God's speech that calls all things into being. 'And God said, "Let there be ...". And there was ...' (Gen. 1). That speech has now taken substantial shape in the Person of Christ, marking the genesis of the new creation, calling forth eternal life, re-fashioning the original image of God in humankind, restoring order to the disordered chaos of man's ignorance and sin.

This is what lies behind the first Advent antiphon. 'O Wisdom, you come forth from the mouth of the Most High. You fill the universe and hold all things together in a strong yet gentle manner.' The Old Testament book of Proverbs, cradling such a desire in its infancy, could only imagine what the Christian Church actually encounters at Christmas. It would never have dared to expect its own poetry to leap from the page and dwell on the earth. 'The Lord by wisdom founded the earth; by understanding he established the heavens; by his knowledge the deeps broke forth ...The Lord created me at the beginning of his work, the first of his acts of old ...When he drew a circle on the face of the deep, I was there ...when he marked out the foundations of the earth, then I was beside him, like a master workman; and I was daily his delight, rejoicing before him always, rejoicing in his inhabited world and delighting in the sons of men' (3:19−20; 8:22; 27; 29−31).

What the writer of Proverbs would not have thought of asking for, Isaiah did. In his moment of extreme anguish at the desperation of Israel he sees only one solution: 'O, that you would tear the heavens open and come down!' (64:1). It was as if God, who inspired the prayer as he inspires all scripture, was so eager to reveal the wisdom of his plan in his Son, that he almost let the secret slip before it was due. In retrospect we can see now a significance that Isaiah did not. What Advent proclaims is that no hope is too daring when compared with the Lord's resolve to rescue his people.

We pray for God's wisdom in Christ because not only did he create all that exists through the Word that proceeds from his mouth; he also 'holds all things together' in him 'in a strong yet gentle manner'. It is through the crucified Word made flesh that he does so. In the christological hymn of Colossians, St Paul draws into unity the entire imagery of the wisdom theme and presents its fulfilment in Christ's passion. 'He is the image of the invisible God, the first-born of all creation; for in him all things were created in heaven and on earth visible and invisible ... All things were created through him and for him ... and in him all things hold together ... Through him (God reconciles) all things to himself, whether on earth or in heaven, making peace by the blood of his cross' (1:15–20).

In Pauline terminology peace and unity are synonymous. The peace that God's wisdom brings is the unity of all things with God and with each other through the reconciling blood of Jesus. The same idea predominated in the post-apostolic writings. The *Pax Romana* ensured the communion of all the Christian communities with each other through their common unity with the church at Rome. Sharing the one way of life in doctrine and practice, they shared in the fruits of Christ's act of redemption. It was a communion that was celebrated at the Eucharist. All who lived in peace with Peter's successor enjoyed eucharistic hospitality at each other's table. It was the sign of the restoration of fellowship which the foolishness of Adam interrupted. It was the sign of the cross. For Paul too the Lord's Supper was the efficacious proclamation of 'the Lord's death until he comes' (1 Cor. 11:26). It was therefore also the means towards, as well as the expression of, Christian fellowship and holiness. 'Because there is one bread, we who are many are one body, for we all partake of the one bread' for after all, 'The bread which we break, is it not a participation in the body of Christ? The cup of blessing which we bless, is it not a participation in the blood of Christ?' (1 Cor. 10:17; 16).

Paul's reflections were directed to a faith-family at Corinth that experienced a lack of unity. It was tragically fractured and flawed by serious divisions caused by elitism, spiritual pride, social distinction, sexual immorality and doctrinal heresy. All the problems that church communities still suffer today. This is the disorder that Christ enters into as Wisdom personified, to change. This is where he desires to 'hold all things together' again. Not abandoning his people, but bearing his cross among them, teaching the members of his mystical body to recognize in their scars of division and sin the wounds imprinted on his historical flesh which, even at the resurrection, remain to inspire faith in his love. 'He himself bore our sins in his body on the tree, that we might die to sin and live to righteousness. By his wounds you have been healed' (1 Pet. 2:24). Paul's advice to the Corinthians − 'Let a man examine himself, and so eat of the bread and drink of the cup' (1 Cor. 11:28) − was a call back to the Eucharist. For it is in the sacrament of Christ's death that the wisdom of the gospel, of the incarnation, of the cross enters into the believing community, inserting its members into Christ himself, conforming them to the wisdom of God's word, God's will.

In Israel's Wisdom literature such access to God was memorably depicted in terms of a meal. 'Wisdom has slaughtered her beasts, she has mixed her wine, she has also set her table ... To him who is without sense she says, "Come, eat of my bread and drink of the wine I have mixed. Leave simpleness, and live, and walk in the way of insight"' (Prov. 9:2−6). It was imagery that Jesus loved and incorporated into his message, and instituted in reality as the abiding memorial of his life, death and resurrection. In Matthew's Gospel, when he warned his disciples to 'beware the leaven of the Pharisees', he challenged them in the same breath to perceive the meaning of the multiplication of the loaves. 'Then they understood that he did not tell them to beware of the leaven of bread, but of the teaching of the Pharisees and Sadducees' (16:5−12). They also understood at that moment that his feeding the four thousand and the five thousand referred to his instruction of the crowds. The nourishment he offered was of the heart and mind, wherein he recognized and served the greater hunger.

The connection between bread and word is made explicit in John chapter six. 'Jesus said to them, "I am the bread of life: he who comes to me will never hunger, and he who believes in me shall never thirst . . . I am the living bread which came down from heaven . . . My flesh is food indeed, and my blood is drink indeed. He who eats my flesh and drinks my blood abides in me and I in him . . . The words that I have spoken to you are spirit and life' (6:35; 55–56; 63). Similarly in Luke's Gospel, the breaking of bread at Emmaus is preceded by a sharing of the word on the road. One event led to the other. In both together the disciples recognized the risen Lord. 'Did not our hearts burn within us while he talked to us on the road, while he opened to us the scriptures?' (24:32). Giving us the pattern of the earliest Christian agape, St Luke identifies the wisdom of Jesus as a gift from heaven which not only enters the ear, not only appears enfleshed among men, but is intended to become part of us, intends that we should become part of him. This extraordinary communion of body and spirit with God's redemptive wisdom is the mystery concealed from before the ages which has now been made known.

In the Eucharist Christ consecrates the entire universe, drawing it into himself and thereby transforming it. All created things, all peoples, are changed in a way that is signified by the substantial change of the eucharistic elements. It bears sacramental witness to the process of what we are becoming. As wheat grows from seed, is turned to flour, becomes bread, becomes the body of Christ; as the grape emerges from the flower, becomes the wine that becomes the blood of Christ, so through the power of the all-wise word made flesh and suffering, are we being transmuted into that which we receive. The Eucharist is the constitutive sacrament of the People of God — it makes the Church the Church. In it are contained all the mysteries of Christ's life, all his divine wisdom. By sharing with us his eucharistic body he is perfecting our membership of his ecclesial body, identifying us more closely with himself until we become so completely one with each other and with God that we embody his wisdom not only in our action but in our very state of grace.

The Eucharist is the Church. The Church is the Eucharist. Each is the real body of Jesus, and he has only one body. What the Sacrament is, the Church is − but extended in time and space. What the Church is, the Eucharist is − but concentrated in the here and now of the liturgical celebration. This is why the Second Vatican Council can rightly say that the Eucharist is the source and summit of the Church's activity, the fount from which all its power flows (*Sacrosanctum Concilium*, §10), and that therefore no other action of the Church can equal it in holiness or fruitfulness (SC, §7). The Wisdom of God resides in the Church, in its eucharistic liturgy, in its celebration of the Word, in its charitable activity. That Wisdom abides at the heart of creation; it is the still, calm centre of the maelstrom of life, giving meaning to all that happens, good and bad, making sense of human destiny by directing all things back to God. 'You fill the entire universe, holding all things together in a strong yet gentle manner.' Advent is therefore both the season of the Coming, and the Becoming. The more Christ comes, the more we become what in his wisdom he is making us. It is the antiphon's express desire that as the eucharistic Church we will be drawn in towards that central Truth which is the fullness of God's plan, not doomed to an endless, purposeless orbit around the distant circumference of falsehood.

The closer we approach true wisdom, the inner centre of Eucharist, the closer we come to each other in the Church. The further we travel in along the radius from the outer perimeter, the narrower grows the gap between people. When all the members of the community converge on Christ at a worthy celebration of the liturgy, they are also at one with one another. This is why we speak of Holy Communion. There is unity here with God and neighbour, a sacramental fulfilment of the gospel. Our oneness with neighbour is effected by our oneness with God. Our oneness with God in Christ is achieved by our common unity with each other. The Eucharist consequently is a sign of things to come. The fulfilment of our communion is as yet sacramental: real though not finalized. There is still the possibility of dis-union through the foolishness of sin. But in this moment of liturgical community we see prefigured the future communion of saints at the end of time. It is, as it were, a retrojection back into the present of what will be at the consummation of the ages, the *arrabon* or pledge of what God has in store for his faithful people when Christ returns.

Even more, the Eucharist is the beginning of that final event. It is the first step of the second coming, the first taste of its consequences. The wisdom that is imparted here, which transforms men and gathers all things into one in a firm yet gentle manner, is the timeless wisdom of eternity, the eschatological victory of Christ already reigning on earth in the Church. It is this which makes the Church, 'although it does not actually include all men, and at times may appear as a small flock' nevertheless 'a most sure seed of unity, hope and salvation for the whole human race' (Vatican Council 11, *Lumen Gentium*, §9). Aware of this, conscious that it already houses in its womb the wisdom that will unite all creatures, the Advent Church prepares for Christ's present and future coming by praying for the unity which is truth. 'O Wisdom ... come to teach us the way of truth.'

This prayer is not just for itself. It is for the entire creation of which the Church is the first-fruit offered to God. It is prayed in the name of every creature under heaven, that all might be subsumed into the eucharistic wisdom of Christ and be presented back to the Father through him, restored to the original perfection in which it was made. If it does not yet see that unity made visible, the Church nevertheless believes that it is already there in mystery, even more glorious than it was at the dawn of time. For now, because it has been saved by Christ, it can boast that it caused the Almighty to reveal himself as Redeemer and Sanctifier as well as Creator. Sin achieved what original grace did not: a chance to measure the immeasurable love of God for men.

With this in mind, how could the worshipping Church ever doubt the fulfilment of Wisdom's plan? If it must wait, it is because it is still in Advent. So it waits vigilantly, as an expectant Church. Just as there can be no Eucharist without sacrifice, so there can be no unity without patience. Patience is a form of suffering. Both words come from the same etymological root. To wait for the Lord patiently is to suffer the human condition, as Jesus suffered it, until that moment when he chooses to bring all things to their completion.

However this suffering is no passive affair. It is the active principle that steers the Church and each of its members through the challenges that history presents to the preaching of the gospel. Established for this very purpose, it now plays the part that Wisdom played metaphorically in Proverbs. Calling on the wise men of every age, it invites all to come to Bethlehem bringing gifts — not of gold, frankincense and myrrh, but the faith, hope and love they signify — and to recognize there the source of all wisdom and its perfection in the Word made flesh, and to pay him homage. With St Paul it cries aloud in the streets, 'Adapt yourselves no longer to the pattern of this present world, but let your minds be remade and your whole nature thus transformed. Then you will be able to discern the will of God, and to know what is good, acceptable, and perfect' (Rom. 12:2. KNOX).

It is to see this accomplished that the universal Church each year recites in unison the first of the 'O' antiphons on December 17th.

Chapter Three

O Adonai

December 18th. O Adonai and leader of Israel, you appeared to Moses in a burning bush and you gave him the Law on Sinai. O come and save us with your mighty power.

What the Church has in mind when it intones this antiphon is the great event of the exodus and all that went with it. The deliverance of the Hebrews from slavery through Moses, the revealing of the divine name, the sealing of the covenant between the Lord and his people, the dictation of the Ten Commandments on tablets of stone at Mount Sinai. It is the magnificent story of the beginning of a nation, its political and religious identity, its struggle for freedom, its search for a homeland. It is also the story of how we began to know God and to learn his purpose for the human race. It speaks to us of the majesty of a Deity who is in control of desperate situations. One who perceives the needs of the oppressed and acts decisively on their behalf. His methods may sometimes be unconventional and perplexing. His timing can appear haphazard, his choice of human instruments downright foolhardy. But always he is One who can be trusted because he is motivated by utter love of his chosen ones and therefore has their best interest at heart.

We recall the exodus today because we recognize in these beginnings of Israelite history a type of the salvation brought to us by that same God through the child who is born at Christmas. In Christ all the elements of the Old Testament epic are endowed with a new significance when read again in the light of the paschal mystery. Suddenly an underlying plan emerges that is far more ambitious than

30

anything Moses might have imagined. A dazzling brilliance of purpose shines out as the events are interpreted as prototypes, images of a world-wide spiritual liberation. Now it is all men who form the Chosen. The bondage lifted is the yoke of sin. The blood of the lamb is that of the cross. The enemy drowned is the power of Satan, the safe passage is through the waters of baptism. Jesus is the new Moses, his beatitudes the Decalogue of life, his Spirit the principle of the new covenant.

When the Church invokes the Son of God in terms of the exodus and under the title 'Adonai and leader of Israel', it is calling down all the force of that first deliverance upon the present moment of history. It is asking again for a precise understanding of its spiritual fulfilment as it ponders the mystery of Christ against the backdrop of God's dealings with his Old Testament people. Not just an understanding of the mind but, even more, of the spirit. It seeks the existential experience of liberation from all that ensnares it. 'O come and save us with your mighty power.' The tone, while joyful and assured as befits the pre-Nativity season, betrays something too of the anguish of the children of Israel at the hands of Pharaoh. For in every age its members toil and strain under the taskmasters of their own limitations. Therefore Christ's coming is necessary and ardently awaited.

Although invoked as 'Leader of (the new) Israel', he is not addressed as 'Moses' but 'O Adonai'. It is an acclamation shot through with the most sacred associations. Translated literally as 'Lord', it was the Hebrew substitute for the Holy Name, YHWH, which was never pronounced aloud. To do so would have been a blasphemy for no lips were clean enough to utter it. Only the high priest, and only once a year on the day of Yom Kippur, had the authority to whisper YHWH's name in the Holy of Holies as he confessed the sins of the nation. When any other Jew unrolled the scrolls in the synagogue on the sabbath and came to the Almighty's name, his eye would see inscribed above it, Adonai – Lord, and this he would read for the congregation instead. Then all present understood that YHWH was meant, though in time few could remember how it even sounded.

The fact that God had voluntarily disclosed his personal name to the people of Moses was considered a sign of infinite graciousness. It meant that he wanted to be known as their God, for them to be seen as his people. YHWH and the Hebrews were now on first name terms. It signified that they were intimate associates. Such is the effect in any society of using the proper name. It gives unrestricted admittance to the person concerned. So with YHWH. The remarkable intimacy he permitted by dropping his formal titles marked an end to the former distance that was appropriate between the transcendent Creator and his creatures. God was now enfolding his children in a loving embrace that invited them to dispense with formality and rest in his ease. This was precisely how the prophet Hosea envisaged the relationship as he later recalled those halcyon days of the exodus. 'When Israel was a child I loved him, and I called my son out of Egypt ... I myself taught Ephraim to walk, I took them in my arms ... I led them with reins of kindness, with leading-strings of love. I was like someone who lifts an infant close against his cheek; stooping down to him I gave him his food' (11:1−5. JB). It was a tenderness of spirit that the psalmist caught perfectly, that he found he could respond to, in his prayer of trust: 'Truly I have set my soul in silence and peace. As a child has rest in its mother's arms, even so my soul' (Ps. 130/131). This knowledge of God also marked the beginning of a new awareness of the Hebrews' own identity. Henceforth they were no longer a disparate conglomeration of Semitic tribes, but a real people, God's Chosen People. Soon to have a law and a land of their own, a culture and religion that was theirs, they looked to YHWH for the protection and guidance they required for their new-found national existence.

Hence it was Israel's intimacy with God that achieved the people's liberation. Deliverance from bondage became a real possibility once they discovered that he was on their side. For him to initiate friendship was to commit himself to setting them free. This is why at the burning bush, the revealing of the divine name coincided with Moses' election to go to Pharaoh and order him to 'Let my people go'. On that occasion Moses had told the Lord that if he was to bring the people with him they must know who it was that sent him. The name was an essential part of the process. There could be no exodus without it.

Its power bestowed competence upon Moses, assembled the people behind him, and neutralized the grip of the oppressor.

At the same time, by entrusting his name into the custody of men God left himself vulnerable. He had put into their hands a force which could be used against him if they chose. Love had compelled him to do this and he did it freely. But such love can never be matched in return. Consequently God exposed himself to the very fate he so abhorred for his sons, and allowed himself to be captivated by his mercy even as he broke the fetters of their captivity in Egypt. The Hebrews realized this themselves. Which is why they developed the custom of never using the name at all. In their moral code the command against doing so was second only to the prohibition on idolatry. The two precepts were akin: first, respect for the Person, then respect for his name. In the Semitic mentality the name and the person were one reality. The name *was* the person. To defile the personal name was to defile the one who bore it. This concept was not foreign to later civilizations. In Anglo-Saxon times for example the precious name of the liege-lord was commonly hidden by his vassals in cryptic runes to protect their leader from the curse of his enemy. Should the secret of that name fall into the hands of the foe they could control his power, diminish his strength, and ultimately kill him. The same principle is at work in voodoo today. How understandable then that God should have begged his people not to take his name in vain! It was a plea that, morally, they ignored.

Although the Hebrew race held God's name in highest esteem, they failed to pay him the reverence that was his due. Hence the broken covenants, the worship of Canaanite idols, and the personal infidelities. They formalized the relationship with YHWH that he had intended to be intimate, and trivialized the spirit of his commandments upon which that intimacy was based. As the prophets and visionaries of Israel were constantly repeating, no People of God could continue to affront the Holy Name and remain free. But no matter how many the prophets and covenant-renewals, Israel's spiritual servitude to sin proved more obdurate than anything they experienced in Egypt.

A lesser god than YHWH would have regretted making such a marriage and wedding his name to so fickle a bride. But then a lesser god would not have condescended to a union with men which left him so vulnerable. YHWH did so in the foreknowledge that his name would be betrayed. He also knew what this betrayal foreshadowed: the crucifixion of that Divine Name made flesh in Jesus of Nazareth. And yet the plan went on because it was precisely by the multiple rejections of his name, culminating in the death of Jesus, that every kind of slavery would be crushed and defeated. Not only the political enslavements of God's people but their spiritual and moral slavery as well.

This is why the Church in Advent calls upon the coming Christ as 'O Adonai'. It is a direct application of the Holy Name, in its covert form, to Mary's son. One of the earliest Christian faith-formulas was 'Jesus is Lord'. 'If you confess with your lips that Jesus is Lord and believe in your heart that God raised him from the dead', wrote St Paul to the Romans, 'you will be saved' (10:9). It was the great and sustaining creed of the post-resurrection Church at Pentecost, when the full redeeming significance of Jesus' name burst forth upon the Christian community like light from heaven, like a terrific fire that burned and yet never consumed. 'Know assuredly,' cried the apostle Peter in his Pentecost sermon, 'that this Jesus, delivered up according to the definite plan and foreknowledge of God, God has made both Lord and Christ, Leader and Saviour' (Acts 2:23, 36; 5:31). Not by accident was Jesus crucified, nor by the whim of tragic fate, but by deliberate, pre-destined design, in order that sin might be forgiven through the name of Jesus Christ, and the Spirit of that name be poured out and received (Acts 2:38).

At Calvary men nailed both the name and the Person of Jesus to a tree. It was the ultimate rejection of God's very Self, nominally and personally, in a series of rejections that included all the apostasies of the past. But this time it was done by Jew and Gentile together, Hebrew and Roman. The name they hammered up above the head of the Crucified, and scoffed. The Person they pinned up by the wrists and mocked. That open scroll above, which desecrated a name so holy that its Old Testament counterpart was never even uttered, gave silent explication of the desecration that was happening below. YHWH was completing, through his Son's patient endurance, the disclosure of his true identity to his people. For in Jesus' open arms on the cross, as in the open scroll above, God intentionally exposed his soft under-belly, the most tender and intimate part of himself, and allowed men to take abject advantage of his awesome vulnerability by piercing Jesus' side with a lance. It was to the supreme advantage of mankind's salvation that they did so.

As St Paul explained to the Philippians, because Christ suffered the degradation of sin 'therefore God has highly exalted him and bestowed on him the name which is above every name, that at the name of Jesus every knee should bow, in heaven and on earth and under the earth, and every tongue confess that Jesus Christ is Lord, to the glory of God the father' (2:9−11). This was the message of Pentecost which the apostles saw so clearly and which so intoxicated them with joy that they were taken for drunken men. 'There is salvation in no one else,' they proclaimed, 'for there is no other name under heaven given among men by which we must be saved' (Acts 4:12). Two thousand years later the Church is still echoing Peter and Paul's affirmation: that in Jesus born of Mary, the power of God's name, first revealed to Moses in shadows cast by the flames of the burning bush, has been stunningly unleashed for good in the full splendour of its breathtaking simplicity and humility. In Christ crucified, the intimacy initiated with the people of Israel for their liberation and nationhood, is given to us naked and bleeding for our deliverance from damnation, for our election to the kingdom of heaven. 'For you have made us a kingdom and priests to our God, and we shall reign on earth' (Rev. 5:10).

The Lordship of Jesus was a Pentecost message because it required an outpouring of the Holy Spirit to open the eyes of faith to the meaning of what had happened to Christ. St Paul assured the Corinthians, 'No one can say "Jesus is Lord" except by the Holy Spirit' (1 Cor. 12:3). The cross was the humiliation of Jesus' name; his resurrection made it exalted; by his ascension was it glorified. That is, by his return to life, by his return to the Father, Lordship was bestowed upon the name that identified Jesus as Suffering Servant. But Pentecost was the moment when full comprehension dawned upon the new believers with the force of the midday sun. It was a morning event – at nine o'clock am – yet the Spirit's enlightenment, like the noon-tide heat that dispels the dew, annihilated all illusions, misapprehensions, and traumatic tensions that still obstructed the faith of Jesus' disciples. No longer would they ask, 'Lord, will you at this time restore the kingdom to Israel?' (Acts 1:6), nor would they be accused of speechless incomprehension: 'Men of Galilee, why do you stand looking into heaven?' (Acts 1:11). They now understood that the Kingdom won by Jesus was of a different kind from what they previously expected, that his messianic lordship was not of a political or military nature, and that his return to them – which they had anticipated as a return to how things had been before – was in fact accomplished in this descent upon them of 'power from on high' (Luke 24:49; Acts 1:8).

Pentecost was originally a Jewish feast, which is why Jerusalem was crowded at that time with pilgrims and visitors from abroad, 'devout men from every nation under heaven' (Acts 2:5). It was the Israelite celebration of the giving of the Law to Moses at Mount Sinai and the ratification of the covenant. This event occurred fifty days after the Hebrew Passover which initiated the exodus. The two feasts were linked. The God who revealed his name and led his people out of slavery was the same who forged the great alliance with them and solidified it in the prescripts of the Decalogue. His commandments were as solid as the stone they were written on, and religious Jews treasured them as the founding rock of their faith.

The Advent antiphon's supplication – 'O Adonai, you gave the Law on Sinai. O come and save us with your mighty power' – is not however for the Jewish law or the Mosaic covenant. It is for the reality that these things signified and which came to pass at Christian Pentecost: the new covenant, the new law which is now inscribed not on tablets of stone but on human hearts. This was what the prophet Jeremiah had declared would come about in the latter days, in the age of Messiah. 'Behold, the days are coming, says the Lord, when I will make a new covenant with the house of Israel and the house of Judah, not like the covenant I made with their fathers when I took them by the hand to bring them out of the land of Egypt, my covenant which they broke, though I was their husband, says the Lord. But this is the covenant which I will make with the house of Israel after those days, says the Lord: I will put my law within them, and I will write it upon their hearts; and I will be their God and they shall be my people' (31:31−33). The waiting Church of Advent today keeps these words in mind as it imitates the first disciples of the Acts who waited in the upper room for this promise from the Father to appear. Christmas therefore is a type of Pentecost. Men awaiting a birth. The birth of the Lord in a stable. The birth of the Church in an upper room in Jerusalem. The re-birth of hearts in a fiery baptism of the Spirit, God's 'mighty power' sent in response to the prayer, 'O come and save us'.

What is imprinted on the human soul by this coming − the New Testament covenant and law − is the passion, resurrection and glorification of the sacred name of Jesus, Lord and Christ, whose paschal mystery seals the intimacy between God and us that God always desired for our true freedom. That freedom was never possible under the Jewish legal code. In itself it was really another bondage because it could not be kept without the Spirit. Moreover it was not in itself complete until Jesus came and fulfilled it by his teaching on love and his death on the cross. Before the Word became flesh and the Spirit was poured out, the Sinai charter could do no more than lead men to expect what was yet to come. It merely highlighted sin, it could not remove it. Therefore 'the law was our custodian until Christ came . . . we were confined under the law, kept under restraint (by it)', said St Paul (Gal. 3:24; 23). His language is that of imprisonment. The old dispensation was for a people who were still children, minors awaiting the age of maturity before coming into their rightful inheritance (Gal. 4:1−3), captives still, in their ways, to a nature yet unredeemed.

The followers of Moses of course did not see it that way. For them the Law was the most precious gift God had to give. They boasted among the nations of the singular privilege they alone had received. 'He makes his word known to

Jacob, to Israel his laws and decrees. He has not dealt thus with other nations; he has not taught them his decrees' (Ps. 147). All the imagery surrounding the Law is of light. Not only the brilliance of the burning bush but also the volcanic fire of Sinai as it erupted in majesty and glory when Moses ascended to YHWH to receive the ordinances on stone. Centuries later the author of Wisdom recalled the plague of darkness in Egypt which affected all but the children of Israel. Why was it, he asks, that while the Egyptians stumbled in impenetrable night yet 'for Thy holy ones there was very great light' (18:1)? The answer was as clear as the day: 'For their enemies deserved to be deprived of light and imprisoned in darkness, those who had kept thy sons imprisoned, through whom the imperishable light of the law was to be given to the world' (18:4). It was said that even the skin of Moses' face was transfigured by the glory of this light so that when he came down from the mountain the people were afraid to approach him, so radiant was the directive he had seen (Exod. 34:29–35).

In comparison with what they had before, the Hebrew Law was indeed a magnificent achievement. It made possible the construction of a social order to serve the needs of a sedentary society after its nomadic wanderings. It provided stability against greed and oppression from within, and a format for dealing with enemies from without. It was fair to the weak and just to the rich. It curbed unrestrained retaliation for injustices done, and set up a workable system of redress for injury inflicted. But it did not bring holiness. In time it paved the way for the cunning and the clever to manipulate and sharp-shoot to the advantage of the baser human instincts, so that by the time of Jesus he was compelled to warn his fellow Jews that 'unless your right-eousness exceeds that of the scribes and Pharisees, you will never enter the kingdom of heaven' (Matt. 5:20).   Therefore although it was useful for a time – from Moses to Jesus – and served its purpose well, it was not in itself God's last word to the people he had freed from earthly bondage. It was not, to use St Paul's term again, the inheritance left for the children in their Father's will. For that a death had to occur, the divine Sonship had to be extended to a host of members, the family had to come of age, be imbued with

the spirit of adulthood. In Jesus' coming that time was fulfilled. His death and resurrection perfectly met the terms of
the will and at Pentecost the inheritance was released.

Now the children were free to enter upon the good things
promised. They no longer had to negotiate for their live-
lihood, drawing up useless invoices, bonds and bills that
could not be made good: the temple sacrifices of bulls
and goats, rules about circumcision, dietary laws, feast and
rituals. The reality, of which these things were merely the
legal tender, was the precious blood of Christ which simultaneously repaid the debt owing to God by men *and* conferred
the benefit held in trust for them, with immediate effect.

Nobody saw and understood this more clearly than Paul.
In his Jewish days he had been a Pharisee of the most committed kind. Educated in the traditions of his fathers under
Gamaliel in Jerusalem − the Hebrew finishing-school *par
excellence* − his intellectual grasp of the Mosaic religion was
of the highest calibre and his observance of the law impec-
cable. Yet after his conversion he was to write: 'Whatever
gain I had, I counted as loss because of the surpassing worth
of knowing Christ Jesus my Lord. For his sake I have suffered the loss of all things, and count them as refuse, in
order that I may gain Christ and be found in him, not
having a righteousness of my own, based on law, but that
which is through faith in Christ, the righteousness from God
that depends on faith; that I may know him and the power
of his resurrection, and may share his sufferings, becoming
like him in his death, that if possible I may attain the resurrection from the dead' (Phil. 3:7−11). The bright light that
surrounded him on the road to Damascus and threw him to
the ground was a metaphor for Paul's Pentecost. It left him
physically blinded for three days − an interlude of paschal
significance − until his baptism by Ananias and his new life
of preaching the gospel. This blindness brought a fullness of
sight to Paul that he never had when he could see. Ironically,
he had to become blind to all that he followed as Saul, to
attain the spiritual vision of Paul. He had to be knocked
off his feet as the Pharisee to find the solid ground of his
faith and authority as the Apostle.

Retaining the imagery of light, he was able to explain the
difference between the old covenant and the new to his

fellow Jews who had become Christians at Corinth but stood in danger of falling back again into the legal traditions of their former religion. 'If the dispensation of death, carved in letters of stone, came with such splendour ... will not the dispensation of the Spirit be attended with greater splendour? For if there was splendour in the dispensation of condemnation, the dispensation of righteousness must far exceed it in splendour. Indeed, in this case, what once had splendour has come to have no splendour at all, because of the splendour that surpasses it. For if what faded away came with splendour, what is permanent must have much more splendour' (2 Cor. 3:7–11).

The fading brightness was a reference to the radiant face of Moses on Sinai. It could not last any more than the Sinaitic covenant could last because it brought with it 'death' and 'condemnation', 'for the written code kills, but the Spirit gives life' (2 Cor. 3:6). The Israelites who accepted the written code with reverence and awe were still subject to the fear of death because they were still ensnared by death's root, their sin. Therefore they were not free. Their minds, like the face of Moses which was veiled to disguise the fading of its splendour, were veiled with ignorance of the truth that brings an end to sin and death. 'But when a man turns to the Lord', Paul affirmed, 'the veil is removed. Now the Lord is the Spirit, and where the Spirit of the Lord is, there is freedom' (2 Cor. 3:17). This is the gift God gives in full to his children in Christ. 'We all', Paul concludes, differentiating the community of the Spirit from that of the law, 'with unveiled face, beholding the glory of the Lord, are being changed into his likeness from one degree of glory to another' (2 Cor. 3:18).

This is what Christmas is about. The concluding prayer of the Divine Office for December 18th sums up the matter entirely. 'By the long-awaited coming of your new-born Son deliver us, Lord, from the age-old bondage of sin.' Share with us afresh the eternal glory of the Spirit, in whom we proclaim Jesus as Lord; let us experience the re-birth of his birth in our patterns of living, which no law can supply. Put your law of love into our hearts that we might never need any rule to regulate our filial intimacy with you, which is holiness. By his incarnation dispel the fear of death which is fed by the consciousness of sin. Let Christ's acceptance of death on our behalf, for which he was born and by which the new covenant is established forever, give us courage to die with him in order to share his resurrection both here and hereafter.

Does this imply that Christians are then above a moral code? Are they to ignore ethical directions and act without reference to the principle of right and wrong? Hardly. The new covenant, in surpassing the law of Moses, did not surpass the common obligation to choose good and avoid evil. Writing on this subject towards the end of the second century, Irenaeus was very precise. 'By the new covenant of liberty God cancelled those provisions, statutes and ordinances which he had given to his people to enslave them and serve the purpose of a sign. At the same time the laws, which are natural and appropriate to free men and are applicable to all without distinction, were amplified and widened, extended and augmented. Out of the abundance of his love, without grudging, God adopted men as sons, and granted that they might know God as Father and love him with all their heart, and follow his Word without turning aside' (*Against the Heresies*, Bk. 4).

The purpose of the New Testament therefore was to raise men's minds above the mentality which equated salvation with moral rectitude alone: the idea that heaven is gained simply by not breaking the rules, and that God cannot close us out if our ethical record is intact. Christianity is not primarily about ethics. It is about relationships. It is the gracious invitation to respond to love by loving in return. No law can achieve this, only grace. When grace is given – indeed lavishly poured out – God's divine love transforms the human being psychologically, spiritually, even physically. 'This is the love I mean', wrote St John, 'not our love for God, but God's love for us when he sent his Son to be the sacrifice that takes our sins away' (1 John 4:10. JB). To see oneself as deeply cherished in the heart of the Trinity is to see everything differently: the world we live in, other people, our life's purpose. It is to discover one's best and truest self, reflected – as it were – in the pupil of God's eyes, full of dignity and worth, shining with the brightness of God himself and therefore like him. 'My dear people' –

St John again – 'we are already the children of God but what we are to be in the future has not yet been revealed; all we know is, that when it is revealed we shall be like him because we shall see him as he really is' (1 John 3:2. JB). This is the splendour that St Paul was referring to, which does not grow dim and which, in our beholding it, changes us 'into his likeness from one degree of glory to another' (2 Cor. 3:18).

It is this revolution in seeing, essentially an experience of faith, that activates the loving response. From this everything else flows, including the moral life which is no longer an imposition of law but the logical consequence of love. Christian morality is not an end in itself. It is the practical means by which divine love is reflected back again, like a ray of light, in human ways. Which is why it is characteristic only of those who are free. Those who pray the 'O Adonai' antiphon of December 18th are the ones who already recognize in themselves the freedom they request. Their prayer articulates also the recognition that, like the Christian converts at Corinth, we are always in danger of falling back from the life of grace into a moralistic framework of fear which diminishes faith and impoverishes love. Then the motivation for acting changes from a desire for intimacy with the Lord to a primitive dread of his judgement. Such a backward step is neither in keeping with the spirit of the old dispensation nor the substance of the new. The birth of Jesus the Lord is about stepping forward out of the self-imposed shackles that men drag after them, and rejoicing with St Paul in the glad assurance that 'there is now no condemnation for those who are in Christ Jesus. For the law of the Spirit of life in Christ Jesus has set me free from the law of sin and death. For God has done what the law, weakened by the flesh, could not do: sending his own Son in the likeness of sinful flesh and for sin, he condemned sin in the flesh, in order that the just requirement of the law might be fulfilled in us, who walk not according to the flesh but according to the Spirit' (Rom. 8:1–4).

Chapter Four

O Root of Jesse

December 19th. O Root of Jesse, you stand as a signal
for the nations;
kings fall silent before you whom the peoples acclaim.
O come to deliver us, and do not delay.

Christmas is the season for fulfilling promises within the
family. Which makes it a feast in which children are particularly prominent. Their unlimited expectations make it
impossible for parents to ignore the requirement of gifts, the
careful concealment of surprises till the right moment, the
stealthy placement of mysterious parcels under the fir tree
by night. Subconsciously it is probably a response to the fact
that children are themselves a promise fulfilled. They carry
the family name, will continue the line. They are the future
that blesses the efforts of the past. They ensure a kind of
immortality. Especially where there is an only child. Then
all the family hopes are concentrated upon him.

Among the Jews of old this was very much the case.
From the patriarchs to the tribal families and Houses, the
great names of the Jewish race were cherished and pre-
served and increased with care and pride. Not to have
children was considered a curse. To generate sons was a
sign of heaven's favour. But this was especially so where
the House of David was concerned. It was to David's line
that the promise made to Abraham was to pass down
through the generations, the promise of Messiah. Therefore
all Israel stood to benefit from the prosperity of David's
family. Should catastrophe strike his House the whole nation
would fall. Upon David's welfare depended the continuity
of God's pledge to send one who would deliver his people

43

from their enemies in a final victory that would bring a lasting peace.

From time to time in their history the nation came close to annihilation. The kingdom of David had its back broken during the Assyrian invasion of the north, and was literally reduced to rubble at the Babylonian exile a couple of centuries later. There were times when the Hebrews seriously wondered if their history was over for there seemed little possibility of any pledges being kept when the nation was in ruins. Yet they survived because God always keeps his word. Both then and now. It is a truth that we have come to live with: our God is a reliable keeper of promises to his children, and those promises are never so secure as when they appear most unlikely to befulfilled.

This is what the 'Root of Jesse' antiphon reminds us about.

Jesse was the father of David. To speak of the House of Jesse is to mean the lineage of King David. David son of Jesse, son of Judah, son of Jacob, son of Isaac, son of Abraham. 'I will make of you a great nation', the Lord had said to Abraham, 'and I will bless you, and make your name great, so that you will be a blessing. And by you all the families of the earth shall bless themselves' (Gen. 12:2–3). A thousand years later that oath was reiterated through the prophet Nathan to David. 'Go and tell my servant David, "Thus says the Lord: I will make for you a great name, like the name of the great ones of the earth ... The Lord will make you a house. When your days are fulfilled and you have lied down with your fathers, I will raise up your offspring after you, who shall come forth from your body, and I will establish his kingdom ... I will be his father, and he shall be my son ... And your house and your kingdom shall be made sure for ever before me; your throne shall be established for ever"' (2 Sam. 7:5, 9, 11–12, 14, 16).

In both instances it was an incredible promise, so magnanimous as to require real faith to accept. According to the myth Abraham was ninety-nine years old and his wife Sarah ninety before their child was conceived. The son of David's promise was born of Bathsheba with whom David committed adultery before murdering her husband, Uriah, by deliberately exposing him to the enemy on the battlefield.

In the face of such odds, against nature and grace, how was the sublime generosity of the Holy One to endure? Yet it did. When another millennium passed, the angel Gabriel was sent to 'a virgin betrothed to a man whose name was Joseph, of the house of David; ... and the angel said to her, "Behold, you will conceive in your womb and bear a son, and you shall call his name Jesus. He will be great, and will be called the Son of the Most High; and the Lord will give him the throne of his father David, and he will reign over the house of Jacob for ever; and of his kingdom there will be no end"' (Luke 2: 26–33). That this child was of David's line St Luke leaves no doubt just as the Letter to the Galatians leaves no doubt that he was also of Abraham's. 'Now the promises were made to Abraham and to his offspring. It does not say, "And to offsprings," referring to many; but, referring to one, "And to your offspring," which is Christ' (3:16).

Together Abraham and David epitomized the hopes of the nation for a Leader whom God would send to deliver his people from destruction. Like Abraham he would father Israel again and increase his house. Like David he would protect and consolidate the kingdom. Like both he would strengthen the religious faith of the people and unite them under a single standard dedicated to YHWH. The country secured by Abraham's faith would be home once more to all the scattered Israelites; the temple planned by David and provided for by him before his death would house again the divine Presence in Jerusalem. God and his Messiah and his people, unmolested and at peace, the envy of the nations, secure from the ravages of war, famine, disease, and fear. What a dream! But no illusion, for YHWH had promised.

While David's house reigned such a future seemed assured. David himself was a leader of genius. Under his military supremacy and political acumen the country north and south was welded into a flourishing civilization. In his son Solomon's time it sparkled with wisdom and art as well. The great Temple project was undertaken and Israel became the talk of the world. Success begot success and prosperity flowed into it from abroad. But after this the tree was cleft in two. Split across the middle as if struck by a thunder-bolt. And then what remained was hewn to its roots.

Under the weight of the shock the voice of the nation groaned in the psalms of lament.

The enemy has laid waste the whole of the sanctuary.
Your foes have made uproar in your house of prayer;
they have set up their emblems, their foreign emblems,
high above the entrance to the sanctuary.
Their axes have battered the wood of its doors.
They have struck together with hatchet and pickaxe.
O God, they have set your sanctuary on fire:
they have razed and profaned the place where you dwell.
They said in their hearts: 'Let us utterly crush them:
let us burn every shrine of God in the land' (Ps.73/74)

It was the summer of the year 587 BC. On July 29th the fierce Babylonian armies breached the walls of Jerusalem, stormed the city and demolished the national spirit. Several thousand able-bodied Hebrews were rounded up in concentration camps at Ramah and roped one to another. Then they were marched across the desert on a six week journey into captivity in Mesopotamia. As they looked back, wet-eyed, at Jerusalem for the last time they could see the smoke rising from the wreckage of their beloved Temple. Gone were the hopes and dreams their fathers had worked for so hard over a millenium and a half. Vanished was the vision of any future other than the gleaming domes and turrets of hated Babylon, the jewel of the East and their conqueror! The anguish of the psalms again expressed their desolation and despair:

By the rivers of Babylon
there we sat and wept remembering Sion;
on the poplars that grew there we hung up our harps.
O how could we sing the song of the Lord on alien soil?
If I forget you Jerusalem, let my right hand wither!
If I prize not Jerusalem above all my joys! (Ps. 136/137).

Back in their homeland a great wailing arose in Judah. From the women, the children, the elderly, for the loss of husbands, fathers and sons. As the prophet Jeremiah watched them file out of Ramah, traditional burial site of Jacob's wife Rachel, Mother Israel, he thought of the Northern exiles captured a century before by the Assyrians and, envisaging all the victims of his beleaguered country as a single family united in defeat, he attributed the women's tears to Rachel herself in her uneaseful tomb. 'A voice is heard in Ramah, lamentation and bitter weeping. Rachel is weeping for her children; she refuses to be comforted for her children, because they are not' (Jer. 31:15).

Both at home and abroad the broken citizens of David, the unhappy offsprings of Abraham found new meaning in the ancient psalm that now took on a tragically appropriate application:

> God of hosts, bring us back;
> let your face shine on us and we shall be saved.
> You brought a vine out of Egypt; to plant it you drove out the nations.
> Before it you cleared the ground; it took root and spread through the land.
> It stretched out its branches to the sea, to the Great River it stretched out its shoots.
> Then why have you broken down its walls?
> It is plucked by all who pass by. It is ravaged by the boar of the forest, devoured by the beasts of the field.
> God of hosts, visit this vine and protect it
> the vine your right hand has planted.
> Men have burnt it with fire and destroyed it.
> Give us life that we may call upon your name ... we shall never forsake you again (Ps. 79/80)

Perhaps it was this very image of the vine that caused Jeremiah, as he later dictated a compendium of his oracles to his secretary Baruch, to recall something he had read in Isaiah from the time of the Assyrian crisis. 'Behold, the days are coming', remarked the inspired Jeremiah, 'when I (the Lord) will raise up for David a righteous branch, and he shall reign as king and deal wisely, and shall execute justice and righteousness in the land. In his days Judah will be saved, and Israel will dwell securely' (25:5–6. Cf. 33:14–16f.). The vine-stock would flourish again! Only a prophet could have displayed such holy optimism, such confident faith in the face of such a levelling of the nation. This was no vain clutching at straws. It was the serene assurance of one who, having watched the worst happen, could see a new creation emerging from the chaos. The hand of YHWH was acting here in a mysterious way, pruning where men thought he had destroyed, cutting back dead wood that men had taken to be healthy, strengthening the stock which he alone perceived as too weak to support the top-growth of another season. So that when, by a remarkable shift in the balance of world power from Babylon to Persia's favour, the Israelites returned to Judah nearly fifty years later, they found their faith purified by re-rooting, their repentance heavy with fruit, and their religious zeal newly sapped and invigorated.

The top-growth that followed comprised a national revival of Judaism which eliminated the idolatry of the mountain shrines that had so ruined their relationship with YHWH. The Temple was restored and refurbished, even grander than before. There arose a priestly caste that led the people in the worship of God. The synagogue system was extended through their towns and villages — something that was completely new — for regular sabbath liturgy. The law and sacred traditions were collated in written form and edited for their meditation as sacred scripture. And their annual feasts by which the covenant was recalled and ratified were prescribed and implemented so that never again would they forget the God who redeemed them.

During this post-exilic period Zechariah borrowed the tree symbol once again to remind them of God's trustworthiness. 'Behold, I will bring my servant the Branch ... Behold, the man whose name is the Branch, says the Lord of hosts: for he shall grow up in this place, and he shall build the temple of the Lord, and shall bear royal honour, and shall sit and rule upon his throne' (3:8; 6:12–13). The prophecy referred not simply to the immediate restoration of Israel entrusted to Joshua the high priest. It anticipated also the future Messiah who would complete the work now in hand by fulfilling the reality of the new Israel which the present pruned vine as yet only signified.

The poetic imagery of the branch, the shoot, the vine, the tree, was by this time popular prophetic coinage. It did more than express the tragic facts of Israel's political fate. It provided the underlying explanation of these in terms of the therapeutic husbandry of the Holy Vinedresser. At the same time it confirmed the appropriateness of Israel's renascent hope in his indestructible promise through each recurring crisis. Even more — it came to have that distinct messianic significance which makes it so relevant to the New Testament and the Christian understanding of Jesus. Above all other visionaries however it was Isaiah who elaborated the richness of the metaphor, highlighting its usefulness for interpreting the disasters of history positively in terms of something greater to come. To this prophet the symbol revealed a truth that Jesus was to demonstrate eight centuries later: there can be no resurrection, either of an individual or of a community, without first a death to what went before. In a memorable passage that is fertile soil to the Advent themes of patience and hope, and from which the antiphon 'O Root of Jesse' is directly drawn, Isaiah explicitly links the regeneration of God's holy vine with the mysterious person who would reform its future stock by himself springing from the root of David's defeated house.

> There shall come forth a shoot from the stump of Jesse,
> and a branch shall grow out of his roots.
> And the Spirit of the Lord shall rest upon him,
> the spirit of wisdom and understanding,
> the spirit of counsel and might,
> the spirit of knowledge and the fear of the Lord.
> And his delight shall be in the fear of the Lord...
> In that day the root of Jesse shall stand as an ensign to the peoples:
> him shall the nations seek, and his dwellings shall be glorious (11:1−3; 10).

Composed in the later period of the prophet's ministry but inserted early in the final text, the portrait of the shoot is that of a little child. He is set amid the wild animals in an idyllic paradise reminiscent of Eden where the aggressive instinct of the beasts gives way to a climate of harmony and restfulness. The wolf and the lamb, leopard and kid, calf and lion, cow and bear — all the contraries of nature, like the contrary impulses in fallen man — will be reconciled, will lie down and feed together, and 'shall not hurt or destroy in all my holy mountain' (v.9). Their peace will be centred on the presence of the little boy among them — 'a little child shall lead them' (v.6) — for through him 'the earth shall be full of the knowledge of the Lord' (v.9).

A remarkable portrait, considering the Old Testament's belligerent imagery of vengeance elsewhere in the teeth of defeat. And yet the language of battle is not absent here. This person will 'decide with equity' in favour of the poor and the downtrodden; he will 'smite the earth', 'slay the wicked', have righteousness for his gear of war. However the language is stripped of its violence in a most disarming way, for his weapons will be nothing more than the words of his mouth and the breath of his lips! Nothing more will be needed indeed: these weapons will be barbed with the gifts of God's own Spirit — the wisdom, understanding, counsel, fortitude, knowledge, fear of the Lord, by which the Messiah will conquer. Thus he will rout the opposition against him by exercising gentleness and forbearance. He will eliminate every trace of the foe by his forgiveness. In short he will utterly annihilate his enemies by turning them into his friends.

The passage must be read in conjunction with Isaiah's Suffering Servant Songs if we are to form a complete identikit of 'the little child ... the shoot from the stump of Jesse'. This is he who 'grew up before (the Lord) like a young plant, like a root out of dry ground' yet 'without beauty of comeliness' because 'he was despised and rejected by men; a man of sorrows, acquainted with grief' (53:2−3).

Ironically the young sapling upon whom all the hopes of the tree of David rested, who was its only chance of new life and limb, was himself to share the fate of the parent vinestock. Isaiah's vision beheld an appearance 'so marred' that it was 'beyond human semblance', a form so oppressed, afflicted, bruised that it was 'beyond that of the sons of men' (7, 10, 14). And yet he opened not his mouth, like a lamb led to the slaughter, like a sheep to the shearers, cut off from the land of the living, entombed with the wicked, although he himself was innocent.

This however was the standard to which the nations would rally, the ensign to the peoples that Isaiah held aloft to his countrymen's view. Somehow by encapsulating the destruction of the vine in his own body, this shoot would yield a rich grape-crop, would surely 'see the fruit of the travail of his soul and be satisfied' (53:11). His spoil would be the many nations that would stand startled by him, the kings who would shut their mouths through their astonishment at him. For he would be lifted up very high before them, would be exalted in their presence (52:13 – 15). It was to be the exaltation of exquisite pain, the elevation of extreme suffering, the type that makes men fall silent, unable to find words for the pity of it. In this way would the child of David, the tender branch, the young tree conquer the world and propagate the root system of God's people more efficaciously than any mighty cedar of Lebanon could ever do.

In Jesus the prophecy came home to rest. 'I am the true vine', he said, 'you are the branches... And I, when I am lifted up from the earth, will draw all men to myself' thus showing, as St John explained, 'by what death he was to die' (John 15:1; 5. 12:32 – 33). It is with these words in mind, the promise of Christ superimposed on the prophecy of Isaiah and the imagery of Jeremiah and Zechariah, that the Church before Christmas prays, 'O Root of Jesse, you stand as a signal for the nations; kings fall silent before you whom the peoples acclaim. O come and deliver us, and do not delay.'

It is for deliverance from all that is symbolized by the bare branches of winter, the denuded trees of December, the feeling of death in the January air, from the hardship that nature herself must endure before spring, that the Church seeks refuge. For it recognizes in the creation a type of the winter of sin: through its whole community and in its every member the sluggish hibernation of the will, the slowing down of the sap of grace, the lopping off of timber in the high winds of adversity, the shock of perceiving itself stripped to its essence. The great schisms of history, the disunity in the rotting bark of whole communities, the diseased limbs of even prominent members.

And in an age of secularism the falling away of what was healthy: the political undermining of its good works in the name of pluralism; the subtle persecution of the world's benign tolerance of its faith; the low-toned accusation of medievalism, backwardness, of being somewhat out of touch. Worst of all — the insidious corruption of youth, its most vulnerable, sprouting shoots, by the deadly spores in the promiscuous atmosphere of the modern climate.

The Church should not be surprised at any of this. A community that invokes the Lord under the title, 'Root of Jesse', should only expect herself to be reduced. 'My Father is the Vinedresser', Jesus instructed his disciples; 'Every branch that bears no fruit, he takes away, and every branch that does bear fruit he prunes that it may bear more fruit' (John 15:1−2). One could say that the pruning of the Church in the latter half of the twentieth century began with Vatican 11. That was when the Father, in anticipation perhaps of the winds of change that were gathering storm force in society, sheared a great deal of unnecessary foliage to prepare the community for the challenges that gales inevitably bring. Vatican 11 was indeed a return to the roots. It brought us back to the sources of the sap that first engendered the vine — the scriptures, the patristics, the apostolic symbols of faith and the beginnings of Tradition. To refertilize and strengthen the stock, to admit new air into the base of the tree, excessive top-shoots needed to be trimmed. For many who had grown old in the pre-Council ways, and who did not perceive how things were changing in the secular environment, such change was truly a trenchant and painful experience. In the light of what the Church has had to face since, however, one wonders how it would have coped without that pruning.

Both from without and within — although in a different manner — the Christian Vine has been severely cut back but has lost nothing of what it is in the process. On the contrary the evidence is already there of what it has gained, new shoots already apparent in branches which, if smaller, are stronger, more vital. The resurgence of its social teaching, its concern for the poor. An updating in its intellectual life through the new theology, wider use of the scriptures, new forms of prayer. A dynamic sense of community, a specific ecclesiology, a really incredible outreaching between Christians of different denominations, the ecumenical movement. A refreshing diminution of clericalism in favour of lay participation in the Church's ministries. A sincere emphasis on the universal call to holiness coupled with pragmatic programmes of pastoral initiative designed to promote a sense of mission and ministry in every baptized person. Finally, with the decline in peripheral forms of popular piety, a concentrated re-focusing on the centrality of the Eucharist – its celebration and veneration – as the Church's very life, its constitutive sacrament from which flows its entire spiritual treasure of grace.

Such indeed has been the pattern in the fortunes of God's people throughout history. In the nineteenth century the crisis over the loss of the Papal States and the challenge to the Church's apostolic authority was matched, following the first Vatican Council, by a missionary flowering unparalleled since New Testament times. In the sixteenth century the Counter-Reformation spear-headed by Trent brought a consolidation of faith and practice that purified the vine-stock universally and produced a harvest of sanctity that characterized its growth for the next four centuries. Similarly in its infancy. The heresies of the first five centuries compelled the great doctrinal clarifications that intensified the christological understanding of Christians everywhere, and enriched their liturgical response to the Person of Jesus in his human and divine natures.

The same has been true in the history of the Church's bloody persecutions as well. In the Acts of the Apostles St Luke makes it clear that the violent opposition to the Vine in Jerusalem caused a wide scattering of its seeds abroad – first in Syria and then Asia Minor and eventually Europe. With the martyrdom of Stephen and James, the imprisonment of Peter and the arrest of men and women in Damascus, occurred that swift spreading of new roots across the known world 'to the ends of the earth', which marked the primitive community's astonishing vitality. Later in the Roman Empire, when the blood of martyrs became the seed of Christians, the message of the gospel – far from withering under the fierce heat of trial –

travelled vigorously along the imperial roads into every civilization. And so it has been ever since. Where the Church is cut down to its stumps, there the Church flourishes and more.

Writing to those early Christians in Rome St Paul called for harmony among them for that very reason — that the Gentiles might be grafted onto the Vine through the spiritual strength of the few. 'We who are strong ought to bear with the failings of the weak', he wrote; 'Welcome one another, as Christ has welcomed you, for the glory of God ... that together you may with one voice glorify the God and Father of our Lord Jesus Christ (who) became a servant to the circumcised to show God's truthfulness, in order to confirm the promises ... As Isaiah says, "The root of Jesse shall come, he who rises to rule the Gentiles; in him shall the Gentiles hope"' (Rom. 15:1−12). Far from being dismayed by the Jewish rejection of the gospel, Paul recognized in this catastrophe the Church's golden opportunity to fill the earth and make of it the new creation. In this way were the scriptures to be fulfilled and God's universal plan accomplished to save all men. His prolonged meditation on the subject in Romans indeed acknowledged a direct cause and effect. Although Israel's denial of Christ brought him 'great sorrow and unceasing anguish in my heart', yet precisely 'through their trespass salvation has come to the Gentiles ... They have been disobedient in order that ... mercy (be) shown to you ... A hardening has come upon part of Israel, until the full number of the Gentiles come in ... Some of the branches were broken off, and you, a wild olive shoot, were grafted in their place to share the richness of the olive tree . . . (whose) root is holy ... the root that supports you' (Rom. 9:2; 11:11; 31; 25; 17; 16; 18). In the final scene of Acts St Luke dramatizes the mind of the apostle in his concluding speech from his domestic prison in Rome. As the local Jewish leaders depart from their visit to Paul there, unmoved by his lengthy arguments and testimony, unconvinced by his preaching on Jesus 'both from the law and the prophets', his final statement to them sums up also the point Luke himself has been making to Theophilus about the Church and its mission in a time of distress: 'Let it be known to you then that this salvation of God has (successfully) been sent to the Gentiles; they will listen' (28:28). Not despite, but through human opposition, does the shoot spring forth from the tree of Jesse, a scion thrust itself upward from its roots.

Through the sufferings of the Church in the world the cross of Christ thus draws all men to the Lord as he promised. The suffering of Paul over the fate of his fellow Hebrews; the alienation of missionaries and martyrs in every epoch and society; the emarginalization of believers today in their stance against what is unjust, untrue. Gradually the kingdom of God is coming about. It can be perceived only through the eyes of faith. Faith in Christ's promises, 'Lo, I am with you always, to the close of the age' (Matt. 28:20), and 'the powers of death, the gates of hell, shall not prevail against . . . my church' (Matt. 16:18). Without such faith the Church could not survive. It is faith that supplies meaning to human suffering, unlocks a purposefulness within it, makes it bearable, as in the case of St Paul. His pain over the recalcitrant Jews was tempered by the knowledge that their exclusion meant the admission of the pagans into the kingdom. He also believed that when God's mercy had been diffused across the world, the Jews would eventually be included in that mercy before the end. He harboured a vision of a single people of God united in Christ that would be the ultimate fruit of all pruning. Which is why he urged the Roman Christians to bear with one another's shortcomings and preserve harmony in their midst. He was thinking of the heavenly community that would be and wished that none might be excluded because they were weak.

That heavenly community, with which the Bible closes, will be one in which the sufferings of God's people will be recompensed. Exchanging their cross for the tree of life, they will see face to face the One who turned all pain to good account. Those who washed their clothes in the blood of the Lamb, those who came through the great persecution, those who resisted the beast − symbol of evil − preferring to endure all that the Church must, rather than opt for compromise. And in the centre of the new Jerusalem stands the source of the revelation: 'I Jesus have sent my angel to you with this testimony for the churches. I am the root and offspring of David' (Rev. 22:16). Spanning the life of the

Church in heaven with the Church on earth, Jesus unites both communities as the vine unites the ground and sky, the above and below, North and South, East and West, by its prodigious extension. At the end of time, as this last word of scripture affirms, the pruning will be complete. Its effect will have been so to fortify the vine that it will easily support the new heaven in its branches, the new earth in its roots, and the entire company of the blessed as its weighty crop, 'twelve kinds of fruit, yielding its fruit each month' (Rev. 22:2). Until that final consummation, the victory song of the saints and martyrs already round the throne of glory mingles with the hymn of the Advent Church still struggling. 'The Spirit and the Bride say, "Come"' to the offspring of David (Rev. 22:17), or as the liturgy puts it on December 19th, 'O Root of Jesse, you stand as a signal for the nations; O come to deliver us, and do not delay'.

Chapter Five

O Key of David

December 20th. O Key of David, and sceptre of Israel,
what you open no one else can close again;
and what you close no one can open.
O come and lead the captive from prison;
 free those who sit in darkness and in the shadow of
death.

The Bible begins with the closing of one gateway and ends
with the opening of another. After the Fall in Genesis 3,
when 'the Lord God drove out the man from the garden
of Eden, ... at the east of the garden he placed the
cherubim, and a flaming sword which turned every way,
to guard the way to the tree of life' (v.24). In the Apocalypse however the lock is sprung and the curse lifted. 'I
looked, and lo, in heaven an open door! I saw heaven
opened, and behold, (One) whose eyes are like a flame of
fire' (4:1; 19:11—12). Between the first slamming shut and
the final throwing open again, swings the epic narrative of
how the key was recovered that undid man's exclusion from
the divine presence.

Jesus is that key. He is the only one that fits the lock.
Whoever holds him can never be excluded again. Whoever
loses him cannot gain entrance. 'What you open no one can
close again; what you close no one can open.' The fourth of
the seven antiphons invites us to recognize Christ's birth as
the moment when mankind found the lost key to its destiny.
It suggests the cry of joy that prisoners give who, confined
in bleak darkness, suddenly discover that the gaoler has left
his master-key in the door of their cell. All they have to do
is reach between the bars and turn it! 'O come and lead the

57

captive from prison; free those who sit in darkness and in the shadow of death.'

The 'Clavis David' motif is a biblical rarity — at least in the Old Testament — though the idea of the open gateway is not. Which makes its inclusion among the other titles particularly interesting. That it was selected from a myriad alternatives in scripture, many of them much more common, means it must have a special significance for the Advent season. It is taken in fact, once again, from Isaiah. He has a spirited passage where the King's steward, Shebna, is to be relieved of his high office, having fallen from favour. 'Thus says the Lord God of hosts, "I will thrust you from your office, and you will be cast down from your station. In that day I will call my servant Eliakim . . . and I will place on his shoulder the key of the house of David; he shall open, and none shall shut; and he shall shut, and none shall open. And I will fasten him like a peg in a sure place, and he will become a throne of honour to his father's house. And they will hang on him the whole weight of his father's house"' (22:15, 19−20, 22−24).

This key was a symbol of authority at the palace in Jerusalem. In particular it gave power to grant or restrict access to the royal personage. The king's steward had supreme control over the household of his master, and therefore over the diplomatic comings and goings of the city and the whole of Judah. It is this concept of access that makes the Key of David title so useful for the Church's understanding of Jesus. In the Letter to the Ephesians for example St Paul writes, 'Through (Christ) we both (Jews and Gentiles) have access in one Spirit to the Father. So then you are no longer strangers and sojourners, but you are fellow citizens with the saints and members of the household of God' (2:18−19).

In the ancient Middle East such a key was a cumbersome affair, given the system of crossbars and bolts for securing the great doors of fortresses and strongholds. Constructed of solid wood nearly a foot in length, and spiked with metal pins at one end, it was best carried on the shoulder. Eventually it became a visible emblem of weighty office by the very manner in which it was borne. The analogy between the steward's key and the cross of Christ hardly needs to be elucidated. The ironic twist in the image as it is realized in

Jesus indeed gives the heaviness of Eliakim's burden, as well as his strategic role in royal affairs, a particular poignancy which Isaiah never dreamed of but which the New Testament reader sees immediately. St Paul was among the first who attributed the Guardianship of access to the one who carried the wood and nails of the cross. In the chapter from Ephesians already cited, he equates the two explicitly. Our reconciliation with God and admission into the Father's presence is accomplished by the Messiah's sufferings. 'But now in Christ Jesus you who once were far off have been brought near in the blood of Christ' (v.13).

After two thousand years of Christianity, in which the culture of the civilized world has been permeated with the real hope of heaven, it is difficult for the modern Christian to imagine what such access to God meant for the first converts. They expressed its novelty and importance in the doctrine of the Ascension. This cosmological metaphor enabled them to express the paradox of Jesus' absence-and-presence in the world, affirm his divine transcendence (seated at the Father's right hand), and define the new kind of existence that awaits the believer whose present life has been transformed by the gospel. Jesus' access to the Father was absolutely relevant to their own destiny. His ascent completed and explained the paschal mystery. It also guaranteed the Church's future glory as Christ's body: where he the head had preceded them in exaltation, there they the members would one day follow. As St Augustine was to put it a few centuries later, 'Just as he ascended without leaving us, so too we are already with him in heaven, although his promises have not yet been fulfilled in our bodies ... It is he alone who has ascended, since we are in him through grace. This is why no one ... but Christ has ascended: not that the dignity of the head is fused with the body but that the body in its unity is not separated from its head' (Sermon 98: On the Ascension).

The ascension of Christ overshadows the whole gospel. The entire account of Jesus' life and works is interpreted in the light of his glorification. From the very beginning of the story the synoptic writers show their consciousness of his return to God's dwelling place by the way they colour the narrative. In the earliest tradition, attributed to Mark (primary source of Matthew as well), the Messiah's baptism in the Jordan features the spectacular disclosure of Paradise. 'And when he came up out of the water, immediately he saw the heavens opened' (Mark 1:10; Matt. 3:16; Luke 3:21). The descent of the Spirit in the form of a dove and the voice of the Father complete the theophany in which God and man, heaven and earth, are re-united in the Person of the Son. His ultimate passage upwards, up out of the water, up from the tomb, up from Mount Olivet, signifies the upward evolutionary course of mankind's calling. The ascending movement is now feasible for all human beings. Because it is open-ended it has no limits; its destination is eternity itself.

What this tableau also makes clear is that man's ascent is dependent on the passion. Preceding any ascension is the descent of Christ. His coming down from heaven, his humiliation in suffering, his burial in the depths of the earth. All of this, dramatically enacted and ritually symbolized by his plunging into the water of the Jordan river, reveals the secret pattern of the master key which has the power to part the clouds of glory and unlock the gates of salvation. In narrative form the evangelists were simply portraying what the apostolic Church had grasped theologically. 'In saying, "He ascended", what does it mean but that he had also descended into the lower parts of the earth? He who descended is he who also ascended far above all the heavens, that he might fill all things' (Eph. 4:9–10; cf. John 3:13).

In the late Gospel of John, the glorious opening of heaven is even more explicitly allied to the cross. The Johannine crucifixion is the cusp of Jesus' exaltation. Raised up on Golgotha, reigning from the cross-beam, steward of his own fate and ours, bringing his work to its consummation, this is he who in the Apocalypse would boast, 'I have the keys of Death and Hades ... Fear not, I am the first and the last, and the living one; I died, and behold I am alive for evermore' (1:18, 17). Calvary is the moment of the Spirit's outpouring in John (19:30). The voice of the Father acknowledging the mission of the Son is here transferred from the baptism scene at the beginning to the triumphant last days in Holy Week after his victory procession into Jerusalem (John 12:28–33). In the Priestly Prayer of John 17 –

Jesus' last will and testament, the statement of his chosen purpose – he articulates the ascension theme in the same breath as he speaks of his death. 'Father, the hour has come; glorify thy Son that the Son may glorify thee, since thou hast given him power over all flesh, to give eternal life to all whom thou hast given him ... I glorified thee on earth, having accomplished the work which thou gavest me to do; and now, Father, glorify thou me in thy own presence with the glory which I had with thee before the world was made ... Now I am no more in the world, and I am coming to thee ... Now I am coming to thee ... Father, I desire that they also (the disciples), whom thou hast given me, may be with me where I am, to behold my glory which thou hast given me in thy love for me before the foundation of the world' (vv. 1–2; 4–5; 11; 13; 24). And finally, at the resurrection appearance to Mary of Magdala – the affirmation of Christ's total dominion over all the powers of sin and death – his first message and commission to the apostolic community is to announce his ascension to his Father's house of many mansions. 'Jesus said to her, "Do not hold me, for I have not yet ascended to the Father; but go to my brethren and say to them, I am ascending to my Father and your Father, to my God and your God"' (20:17).

For St John – as for Paul – therefore, the movement up and the downward thrust is one action. In the paradoxical world of the Christ event they form the same plan, accomplish the same purpose: the opening of doors that would otherwise remain shut forever. Luke's account of the death of Stephen in the Acts indicates that the early disciples had appropriated this lesson in the pattern of their own lives. As the first Christian martyr is about to be stoned, 'he, full of the Holy Spirit, gazed into heaven and saw the glory of God, and Jesus standing at the right hand of God; and he said, "Behold, I see the heavens opened, and the Son of man standing at the right hand of God"' (7:55–56).

What emerges from this confluence of suffering and glory is the New Testament's recognition that the gates opened by the key of the cross are certainly not the gates of Eden. In sacred scripture the Kingdom of God and the Garden of Eden are radically different concepts. The Kingdom is life lived freely and consciously under the reign of God; the

Garden was no more than a life of infantile unawareness
prior to the formation of adult conscience. Adam's exile
was never meant to end in his returning there. His destiny
was to something greater than a garden of ease. The world
of primeval innocence depicted before the Fall is essentially
a world of ignorance. No man who has left childhood behind
can ever return to its amoral security. Nor should he wish
to. Holiness is the consequence of violent combat with the
existential self confronted with the multiple choices – some
good, some not – that constantly challenge the will. No
one who desires holiness can rest until the engagement has
begun. Not even Jesus. 'I have a baptism to be baptized
with; and how I am constrained until it is accomplished'
(Luke 12:50).

Adult innocence – a much nobler state of grace than
that in children – comes about through personal options
for what is right, made in and through Christ. It is the
fruit therefore of the cross accepted in the fulfilment of the
responsibilities of one's state of life. It is a commitment to
the reality of the here-and-now not as one would like it to
be, but as it actually is. Where such a commitment is abdi-
cated in preference to the fantasy of pleasure or ambition as
the basis of happiness, there the Kingdom is renounced.

Until Christ's coming in the flesh, until his descending-
ascent as Key of David, the human will was locked in the
prison of Adam's illusion. What Jesus opened was the possibility of choosing freely the full truth which God revealed in
him. Because there can be no truth without sacrifice, and no
sacrifice without self-denial, the cross marks man's coming-
of-age, his adulthood. His human nature re-formed into the
shape of Christ's humanity, he is no longer imprisoned by
the tyranny of pleasing himself, which ends in death. He
is empowered to achieve what is pleasing to God, which
ends in life.

This is why Christians proclaim Golgotha as Good News.
Their presence in spirit there means that Adam's children
have now gained access to the Tree of Life from which
they were debarred by the cherubim with the flaming sword
in the Eden myth. No longer is that life sought in some
exotic garden of childish imagining. It is found rather in
him who clarified on Calvary once and for all the redemptive

nature of suffering in the moral and spiritual evolution of the species when, recapitulating the whole of history, he offered to God the sacrifice of his own existence and the existence of all who are inserted into him. What the Advent antiphon joyfully announces, echoing the apocalyptic truth of the gospel, is that in Christ crucified, *homo sapiens* has arrived at the apex of his development. That at Calvary we finally face the truth about ourselves that, in Adam, we closed our eyes to. It tells us that we have found at last, in the first-born of all creation hanging from a tree, the lost prototype in whose image we were in fact created. That in his ascension as first-born from the dead, we have likewise glimpsed the ultimate purpose of our evolution and the means towards completing it. That it is through self-emptying and not self-aggrandizement that we rise up as Christ did out of the dark clay from which we were formed, to become participators in the life-giving breath of the divine nature. Like the first stunned disciples, the Advent Church, metaphorically, stands gazing into the heavens in silent awe at what is yet to come.

This is why Pope St Leo the Great, as he contemplated the significance of the entire paschal mystery, was able to assert that our eyes were 'opened much more happily to the revealed glory of our nature than were the eyes of the first members of our race who were filled with shame at their sin', for in Christ's achievement, '*human nature* was exalted above the dignity of all the creatures of heaven ... to receive an elevation that would have no limit until it was admitted into the eternal Father's dwelling, to share the glorious throne of him with whose nature it had been united in the person of the Son' (Sermon 1: On the Ascension).

Such was Paul's understanding of the mystery too, and his wish for the Church. That through incorporation into the glorified Christ, we should 'all attain to the unity of the faith and of the knowledge of the Son of God, to mature manhood, to the measure of the stature of the fullness of Christ; ... no longer children (but growing) up in every way into him who is the head, into Christ' (Eph. 4:13–15).

According to the New Testament there is an immanence about this process, a here-and-now immediacy to it. The Kingdom whose gates the Lord has opened is not just

a future expectation. It is already present in our midst.
'The kingdom of heaven is at hand', is how the synoptics
expressed it as the ministry of Jesus began (Matt. 3:2; 4:17).
In the mature apostolic writings – the Fourth Gospel, Acts,
and Paul's late letters – the sense of an already realized
eschatology is especially strong. While they never denied
an ultimate consummation at the end of time, yet in some
dynamic way the great influx through the unlocked gates had
already begun. Although Christ would eventually present
human-kind to his Father who would then be all in all
(1 Cor. 15:28), the unexpected delay in the Parousia, his
second coming, demanded a critical re-think as decade suc-
ceeded decade and the cycle of death took its toll among the
baptized in the natural way. What the Key of David made
accessible by ascending must necessarily be accessible now.
The solution that soon gained consensus could only lie in
the mission and life of the Church.

Henceforth the open door imagery is applied consistently
to the enlargement of the community's borders and the personal response of each convert to the message of Christ
and the power of his Spirit. Now the ascension takes place
within. Not in any skyward movement but in the interior
opening of doors formerly locked in man's heart. In the
message to the church at Laodicea, for example, the glorified Lord declares, 'Behold, I stand at the door and knock;
if anyone hears my voice and opens the door, I will come
in to him and eat with him, and he with me' (Rev. 3:20).
Here the closedness was the lukewarm response of the rich
and prosperous. In John chapter 20, it was fear. 'On the
evening of that day (Easter), the first day of the week, the
doors being shut where the disciples were, for fear of the
Jews, Jesus came and stood among them and said to them,
"Peace be with you"' (v. 19). Fear changed to faith, timidity
turned to zeal, and the apostolic mission began.

Wherever the earthly barriers of indifference are removed
by listening to the voice and accepting the word, there the
barriers of heaven disappear as well. The faithful church
of Philadelphia is praised precisely because it has done this
whole-heartedly ('You have kept my word' – Rev. 3:8). To
them is promised support in the hour of trial with the now
familiar speech: 'The words of the holy one, the true one,

who has the key of David, who opens and no one shall shut, who shuts and no one opens ... Behold, I have set before you an open door, which no one is able to shut' (Rev. 3:7 − 8).

It was a truth that Paul actually witnessed in the course of his first missionary journey. No matter who welcomes the message finds life, because the word is the gospel of the cross. Coming back to Syrian Antioch from his success among the pagans at Lystra and Derbe, he and his apostolic helpers 'gathered the church together and declared all that God had done with them, and how he had opened a door of faith to the Gentiles' (Acts 14:27). This opening could not be prevented by any human force, not even by persecution. Great suffering indeed was only to be expected. It was nothing but the turning of the key. This is why he deliberately encouraged and exhorted the newly evangelized communities of Asia Minor earlier, 'saying that through many tribulations we must enter the kingdom of God' (Acts 14:22).

In all of this, the vigorous witness of Paul and Luke and John depicts the Kingdom as the openness of God to man and of men to God in the Church. It is clearly a phenomenon that, at one and the same time, elicits the most passionate opposition and the most passionate acceptance. In the tension created between the two poles, the reign of God vibrates and hums like an electric current. Its megacharge is the Spirit that emanates from the crucified Christ, its generator the transformed humanity of Jesus caught up in consubstantial union with the Father in the same divine nature. The Church is the conductor of this power, its summit reaching into heaven, its other extremity running to the earth. For this Church is not just the horizontal community of men in history. It is more precisely the pre-existent and eternal communion of the Triune Godhead, into whose perfect unity a people of faith has been graciously assembled, admitted and gathered up, following the temporal missions of the second and third divine Persons (cf. Vatican 11, *Lumen Gentium*, §4, citing St Cyprian of Carthage, De Orat. Dom. 23).

The vertical movement towards God is of course worked out on the horizontal plane. If the Church is primarily a

mystery, it is equally a visible, tangible reality; a living body
of many members; human as well as divine; enfleshed in time
and space, as well as of eternity. Because it is composed of
relationships, it is as much a happening as an institution.
The Church occurs where the horizontal crosses the vertical,
where human relationships are intersected by the love of God
incarnate in Christ. Matched together in this way the two
dimensions form the sign of the cross, reproduce the cruciform shape into which the Key of David is fashioned and
cut. Hence heaven's gate is unlocked not by God alone, but
by man and God together, Christ and Paraclete, flesh and
Spirit, humanity and divinity, in history and eternity.

This is one of the first lessons that John's Gospel teaches
us. In chapter one Jesus informs Nathaniel, 'Truly, you will
see heaven opened, and the angels of God ascending and
descending upon the Son of Man' (v.51). It was a reference
to Jacob's ladder, the Patriarch's dream of a new, two-
way line of communication between Israel and the Lord.
God's condescending action complemented by the uplifting
response of his people: the vertical dimension. But it could
only become reality, as John makes clear, at the ground-level
interaction of man with man. And so the Word became flesh
and dwelt among us (v.14): the horizontal dimension. Put
the two together, and the cross inevitably appears.

In Nathaniel the human encounter with God through
Jesus the man transformed dull scepticism into dynamic
faith, curt cynicism into hope. From, 'Can anything good
come out of Nazareth?' (v.46), to 'Rabbi, you are the Son
of God! You are the King of Israel!' (v.49) in a matter of
four short verses! For this Israelite, the door of the Kingdom
swung back with dramatic ease in moments. In some mysterious sense the ascension had already occurred within him.
To change direction like this onto the vertical he had to
encounter Truth as reality, be confronted by it through the
humanity of Christ at the horizontal. Here was the meaning
and purpose of the incarnation: that men might ascend the
ladder to the realm of angels, the same ladder down which
came not only angels, but the Son of God himself. In Jesus,
God and man, that crossing of the two dimensions was so
perfect that it inevitably led to the crucifixion. His entire life
on earth was, after all, intentionally cruciform − majesty

being perfectly crossed with ministry, Lordship with low-liness of heart, magnitude of Being with poverty of spirit. All that he was and did therefore, was fully epitomized in the pattern of Calvary, and according to this pattern was heaven breached for man by man in God.

What this tells us is that we open heaven to each other. It happens when, in Christ's name and for Christ's sake, we unlock another's humanity by the humble revelation of our own. When we step down from the aloofness that intimi-dates and inhibits others from achieving what they are capable of. It was this unholy aloofness that Jesus firmly rejected during his second temptation in the desert. 'The devil took him to the holy city, and set him on the pinnacle of the temple, and said to him, "If you are the Son of God, throw yourself down; for it is written, He will give his angels charge of you"' (Matt. 4:5−6). The ascent to the pinnacle was no ascension; the jumping down again, no incarnation. Each was a diabolical parody of the real thing. What Satan had in mind was to reverse the humanity of Christ by elevating him above the level of the world of sinners to the dizzy heights of self-righteousness. From there he could look down untouched at the whole leprous reality of mankind's spiritual and moral decay. Such was the position which the Pharisees accepted, who 'bind heavy burdens, hard to bear, and lay them on men's shoulders . . . but themselves will not move them with their finger' (Matt. 23:4). They chose for themselves 'place of honour . . . the best seats in the syna-gogues, and salutations in the market places' (Matt. 23:5). Against these Jesus directed a scathing and bitter criticism that he never displayed before the ordinary sinner. 'Woe to you, scribes and Pharisees, hypocrites! Because you shut the kingdom of heaven against men; for you neither enter your-selves, nor allow those who would enter to go in' (Matt. 23:13−14).

For the same reason he refuted the temptation to throw himself down from on high as Satan suggested. He would not win disciples at the cost of bedazzling them with a dra-matic show of divinity. Ostentation was the business of high-minded Religious Officialdom. His descent was to be a hidden affair, gentle and unassuming, that he might attract a following by love. Contrary to the impulses of fallen human

nature, he sought the company of the fallen, was content to
be mistaken for a sinner himself in order to lift others above
the pinnacle of man-made temples, to the dignified heights
of redeemed humanity. This was why, after all, he took his
place in line with the penitents on the banks of the Jordan
when he offered himself for a baptism of repentance at the
hands of John.

It was the simple humanity of Jesus that unlocked the
hearts of those he met. They recognized in him one who
'did not cling to his equality with God as a thing to be
grasped' but became as all men are (Phil. 2:6). Seeing this
opened a new hope of holiness in them − from Nathaniel
and the apostles to Mary Magdalene and the prostitutes.
Sanctity was no longer an unreachable goal. Nor was it to
be confused with the sanctimonious externals of their Jewish
leaders. Heaven was to be found within themselves. They
suddenly grasped what no one had ever told them before:
that to become truly God-like requires only that one become,
like Christ, fully human, fully humane.

What was true in Jesus' time is still true today. The key
that releases hope and permits the heart to soar is on the
outside. It takes another to turn it so that doors will open
on earth and therefore also in heaven. Christians are called
to do what Christ did: to set others free to be themselves
that they might perceive the value of what they are, might
rise above what is false within them and put underfoot all
that hinders growth or is unworthy of them.

What is the key by which we reach others in this way?
Sometimes it may be simply tact, or humour, or praise,
tolerance, affirmation or patience. In each case there is
a cross to be endured, for the price of liberating one's
neighbour is the denial of oneself. In the ultimate, the
key is forgiveness − through which the cross and ascension
become most visible. It is a fact that wherever genuine reconciliation takes place, there the paschal mystery appears in
mystical form and the gates of the Kingdom give way.

This was the pattern from the very beginning of the
Church. Not just in its establishment as the apostolic community reconvened by Easter forgiveness. But also in its
prefigurement as the twelve tribes of Israel. In the Elohist
tradition of Genesis, Joseph − a type of Christ − effects

the reconciliation with the brothers who sold him into Egypt when he is eventually re-united with his father, Jacob. The incident where they meet again reads like a kind of ascension story. As Jacob prepares himself for his son's return, 'Joseph made ready his chariot and went up to meet Israel his father in Goshen; and he presented himself to him, and fell on his neck, and wept on his neck a good while' (46:29). The deeply moving quality of this reunion offers an anthropomorphic insight into that other scene (not accessible to us) of Jesus' return to his beloved Father in the glory which he had with him before the world was made (John 17:5; 24). Later, when Joseph's brothers fear he might renege on the pardon he promised, and remind him of their father's wish that their transgression be forgiven, the patriarch – weeping with sincerity – confirms his former pledge. 'Joseph said to them, "Fear not, for am I in the place of God? ... You meant evil against me; but God meant it for good, to bring it about that many people should be kept alive, as they are today"' (referring to his provision of bread for Israel during the famine) (50:19–20). One is reminded of the comparable scene in the gospels where the risen Christ, appearing to those who had deserted him at his passion, bestows his peace and renews their mission (John 20:19–23; 21:15–19). In both instances the future of the community of God's people was assured, despite the infidelity of its founding members, by the generosity of the brother whose fraternal humanity was able to rise above the fault, thus binding them in a new familial covenant with their common father.

Only natural, then, is the noticeable surge of emotion coming up to Christmas when the 'Clavis David' is acclaimed. The liturgy is reminding us that the Church, by its very constitution, is an efficacious sign of forgiveness; that as Evangelist, it is empowered to put reconciliation within the reach of all. We take seriously the self-identifying words of Paul, 'God ... through Christ reconciled us to himself and gave us the ministry of reconciliation; that is, God was in Christ reconciling the world to himself, not counting their trespasses against them, and entrusting to us the message of reconciliation. So we are ambassadors for Christ' (2 Cor. 5:18–20).

The Church rejoices at the power for good that such a ministry confers, at the many openings for grace placed at its disposal. Conscious that it is entrusted with the power of the keys, has been appointed steward of sacraments that unbind and set free, it reflects with deep and prayerful gratitude on the terms of its commission: 'I give you the keys of the kingdom of heaven, and whatever you bind on earth shall be bound in heaven, and whatever you loose on earth shall be loosed in heaven' (Matt. 16:19); and: 'If you forgive the sins of any, they are forgiven; if you retain the sins of any, they are retained' (John 20:23).

To be able to bring happiness in this way to people is not only a privilege. It is an anticipation of the blessedness of heaven. Especially in the modern world where so many are unhappy within themselves, or in their relationships, or in situations that defeat them. Very often sin is at the heart of these tragedies. Yet who wants to be immured in the pride, the selfishness and dishonesty by which we entomb ourselves? To be aware of these weaknesses makes the problem even worse if we are unable to overcome them. Such awareness can lead to self-hatred. We begin to compare ourselves unfavourably with others. The gulf we find there compounds the sense of isolation. Eventually we feel thoroughly trapped and diminished. Into this self-imposed hell, the Church's simple act of forgiving works as a 'bursting of the gates of bronze', a magnificent demolition of 'the iron bars' (Ps. 107/106:16).

The joy felt by the Church when people are helped by its ministry is more than the emotional satisfaction that comes from doing good. It is more even than the spiritual anticipation of the heavenly future. It is the result of an immediate sense of God's presence within itself, God working his reconciliation through his earthly instrument. As a community of weak human beings, the Church knows that no one can forgive sin but God alone. If therefore sinners are healed and liberated in the midst of sinners and captives, it follows that the glorified Christ himself has come and endorsed once again his apostolic commission to the guardians of the keys. For the community whose state is one of permanent expectancy, the nearness of divine grace moving in its sacramental womb is an experience of particular consolation and great gladness through the Advent season.

The twelfth century Cistercian, Blessed Isaac of Stella, perceived in the forgiveness of sin on earth the perfect accomplishment of this intimate communion between the ascended Lord and his reconciling Church. 'It is for God alone to forgive sins . . . Without Christ, therefore, the Church can forgive no sin; but it is Christ's will to forgive no sin without the Church. The Church can only forgive the sin of one . . . whom Christ has touched; and Christ would not wish to hold forgiven the sin of one who despises the Church . . . For Christ is not whole and entire without the Church, nor the Church without Christ. The whole Christ, the complete Christ, is head and body. That is why he can say: "No one has ascended into heaven, but the Son of man who is in heaven". He is the only man who can forgive sins' (Sermon 11). What this means is that the Key of David is not only Jesus, but Jesus and the Church, or more properly, Jesus-in-his-Church. What he is, the Church is; what he does, the Church does. Together they raise the world up to God, offering it to the Father on the cross, in baptism, in the ascension, through forgiveness. Christ the merciful head in heaven, the Church his merciful body on earth: both unified in the one mediatorship between God and man. Whether this reconciliation happens sacramentally at the hands of ordained ministers or spiritually in the lives of all its members, the raising-up of human being is the hallmark of Christianity, and proof of the Church's inseparability from the Son of God.

Out of this action comes a double blessing. Blessed is the one forgiven, but blessed too is the one who forgives. In elevating his neighbour to a level of respect that his actions may not merit, a man is himself raised up to his fullest dignity as a man. This is why Jesus insisted that the highest form of discipleship is the love of one's enemies. The transforming power of such love, which overcomes hatred and breaks the cycle of revenge, qualifies both parties in a conflict 'to share in the inheritance of the saints in light', and delivers them equally 'from the dominion of darkness . . . to the kingdom of (God's) beloved Son' (Col. 1:12—13).

Such is the Bible's ultimate promise, the final vision of the New Testament. The openness of heaven is so complete that there are twelve gates, not one, each unlocked to accommodate the full complement of the reconcilers and the reconciled. 'The twelve gates were twelve pearls, each of the gates made of a single pearl . . . and the gates shall never be shut by day – and there shall be no night there' (Rev. 21:21; 25). And so the story of salvation ends as it began: with no barriers between God and his creature. As the Advent Church ponders this great disclosure and gazes in hope upwards and into the heavenly city, it is momentarily blinded by the theme of light emanating from the new Jerusalem. What the Key of David has opened shall never be shut by day – and there shall be no night there! 'The city has no need of sun or moon to shine upon it, for the glory of God is its light, and its lamp is the Lamb' (Rev. 21:23). The apocalyptic imagery provides the perfect liturgical transition to the next seasonal antiphon for the Church's meditation on the fifth day of the octave: 'O Rising Sun!'

Chapter Six

O Rising Sun

December 21st. O Rising Sun, you are the splendour of
eternal light
and the sun of justice.
O come and enlighten those who sit in darkness and in
the shadow of death.

The Church hails Christ as the Rising Sun at eventide on
December 21st – the mid-winter solstice and darkest day of
the year. It is the time of night's predominance, when the
darkness seems to have overcome all. The sun is at its fur-
thest remove from the northern hemisphere. It appears to
pause as if in death – but only to return, rising once more
to begin a new cycle in the seasons of life. The timing of the
antiphon is perfect. It reflects the people's hope in the birth
of a child destined to die that he might rise in a dawning that
would conquer darkness forever. His appearance is a celebration of the true feast of Sol Invictus – the Unconquered
Sun, whose brief pause in the tomb for three days would be
followed by an eternal spring. So the unrestrained revelry
of Christian Saturnalia is not, like its old pagan forerunner,
some desperate antidote to the fears of winter. It is a spar-
kling elixir of joyful hope that, as Christ has triumphed over
sin and death, so those he has redeemed will share his victory over every bleakness in the human condition that winter
symbolizes.

It has always been the Church's wise practice to overlay
its feasts on the natural round of the seasons. It is indeed
characteristic of the Judeo-Christian tradition: harmonizing
the spiritual worship of God with the wonderful phases of
his ordered creation. This is why Advent – Christmastide

is such a popular and meaningful festival, deeply sacred and deeply cherished. The rich and variant images of light upon which it draws evoke an affirmative response in the natural man as well as in his believing soul. Very little effort of thought or imagination is required to make such a response. Every living thing gravitates towards the light, shrinks from the dark. The rhythm of life itself rises and falls with the spinning of the year: the sun's daily course, the monthly phases of the moon, the nightly rotation of the constellations. From pre-history nomadic peoples plotted their course by the heavenly movements, timed their journeys by the lengthening days. When they settled as farmers they sowed and reaped in obedience to solstice and equinox, and learned to respect the mystery of life and death that embraced in its great spiral every element of the universe. At the centre of that spiral, leading the entire cosmic dance, was the sun.

Archaeological findings earlier this century at Newgrange in Ireland revealed a unique and fascinating insight into man's instinctive reverence for solar phenomena. A tumulus or burial mound is located there in a loop of the river Boyne in County Meath that is older than Stonehenge by a thousand years. Predating the Bible, it was already ancient when Abraham was born, out-rivalling in antiquity even the pyramids of Egypt by several centuries. In 1963 a carefully constructed aperture was discovered above the lintel of its east-facing entrance, so precisely positioned that on mid-winter's day the slanting rays of the rising sun shine directly through, tracing a ribbon of light along the narrow floor of the passage grave until they hit the back inner wall of the burial chamber itself. Unknown anywhere else in the Megalithic architecture of Western Europe, this earliest example of sophisticated solar alignment implies a highly developed religious response to nature by a primitive civilization. Their cult of the dead, like the plan of their passage grave, was fixed on the observable miracle that annually revitalizes the force of the natural world at the specific moment of the year's turning. The Advent antiphon of December 21st does the very same, in terms of Christian faith.

Like the aperture over the portal at Newgrange, the supplication, 'Veni, O Oriens!', aligns the well-placed hopes of the waiting community eastwards. It focuses faith with neolithic sureness upon the one whose appearance brings resurrection in his rays. Through the openness of prayerful invocation his radiance will penetrate the inner chambers of death where mortal sin once claimed fealty. 'You are the splendour of eternal light ... O come and enlighten those who sit in darkness and in the shadow of death.' More solid is this faith than interlocking slabs of granite, more enduring. It is consolidated, perpetuated in the unity of 'living stones ... built into a spiritual house (which is) God's own people called out of darkness into his marvellous light' (1 Pet. 2:5,9).

In proclaiming Christ as the true light the believing community weds the primitive instincts of natural religion with the truths of Judeo-Christian revelation. The signs of God's hand in the created universe and the signs of his personal presence through and in his Son are splendidly integrated through faith. What the natural reason always led men to suspect is confirmed and elaborated in the birth of Jesus. Whatever was misconstrued by the ignorant blundering of the pagan intellect, darkened by original sin, is now corrected and clarified in the fullness of God's self-disclosure at the incarnation. This is why Christianity has never rejected the religious instinct, however pagan, of the people it evangelized, but has always used the elements of the old religions as a basis for introducing the new. The high crosses of Celtic spirituality are a case in point. When Patrick and his followers promoted the gospel in the Ireland of burial mounds, druids, and solar worship, they baptized the former customs as well as the newly-believing converts. Thus instead of obliterating all traces of native awe at winter sunrise, they Christianized the cult of the sun by drawing a cross in front of it. In this way they corrected the error of idolizing any element of creation by pointing to the true God whom the elements themselves proclaim by their very existence and nature. Now the high crosses of Ireland eloquently remind the passer-by in a simple and artistic manner of the theme dear to the heart of John's Gospel and Letters — that Christ is the light of the world and that in him there is no darkness at all (John 9:5; 1 John 1:5). The success of this early catechesis is evident even today. In every cemetery across the country the Celtic cross with its solar circle haloing the wood of our redemption marks the burial site of those who understood and accepted the resurrection of Jesus, and lie quietly awaiting their own. 'O come and enlighten those who sit in darkness and in the shadow of death.'

The early Italian churches dealt with the pagan problem with similarly successful ingenuity. They found that the newly baptized, on leaving the sanctuary after a morning eucharist, would bow reverently to the golden orb of the day that straddled the eastern portal of the building. Old ways die hard even among the most committed! So the presbyters had a fresco of Jesus − 'I am the bright morning star' (Rev. 22:16) − displayed upon the space above the entrance on the inside, so that all who lifted their face to pay homage to the sun would recall that Jesus is Lord. They would be reminded of his words to the faithful at Thyatira, his warning to shun idolatry, and his promise, '(To him) who conquers and keeps my works to the end, I will give him the morning star . . . even as I myself have received power from my Father' (Rev. 2:26−28). Long after this problem had ceased the practice of decorating the inside exits of churches with icons of Christ remained, as is evidenced in the Vatican basilica today.

The gentle and gracious way in which those first converts were led by the teaching and worshipping Church to the truth − not by vicious rejection of the natural instinct but by its proper development and incorporation into Christ − is in itself an effect of the Word's becoming flesh, the humanization of God. By his acceptance of human nature the Son took to himself the whole of creation, restoring it to its original dignity by giving it again its true meaning and purpose. All things were created to give glory to the Creator and to assist man's conscious adoration of the One who made him. The Advent supplication − 'O Come and enlighten' − acknowledges that without the grace of Christmas people would still confuse the creature for the Creator, would still risk losing the very point of their existence by misinterpreting the purpose of the natural order. It also underlines the fact that in Christ's birth, that ancient but recurring error stands corrected. On this theme St Anselm was most articulate. Taking his starting-point from the Virgin Mary's plenitude of grace, he addresses the Mother of God as the one in whom God's recapitulation of all things in their proper order begins.

Sky, stars, earth, day, night, and all things that are meant to serve man and be for his good rejoice because of you, our Lady. Through you they have in a way come back to life, enriched with a new grace. When they lost the noble purpose of their nature, for which they had been made, of serving and helping those who praise God, they were like dead things. They were crushed, disfigured, and abused by idol worshippers for whom they had not been made. They rejoice now as if they had come to life again. Now they are made beautiful because they serve and are used by those who believe in God.

A new and priceless grace has made them almost leap for joy. They have not merely felt God himself, their creator, ruling them invisibly from above, but they have seen him visibly within themselves using them in his work of sanctification . . .

Through the one glorious son of your glorious virginity all the just who died before his life-giving death rejoice that their captivity has been ended (Oratio 52).

It is worth remarking how St Anselm here equates the end of astro idol-worship with the deliverance of the just from death. His oration echoes the mid-winter antiphon. It mirrors in reverse the heathen mistake of coupling the two. In all cases however − whether in the Christian affirmation or in the druidic misconception of the truth − the human religious spirit is profoundly positive in its instinct that life does not end at death. In this it stands against the nihilism that sees only darkness, that denies the purposefulness of creation, argues the absurdity of human existence, and suggests an accidental or fatalistic cause for all that is. By attributing to the rejuvenation of the seasons a credible reason for imagining the same in mankind, the religious faculty on the other hand implies that each moment in life is charged with an eternal significance. That nothing is purely haphazard or isolated from the universal scheme of things. Everything is related to everything else and all are related to the centre as in the great gyration of the natural elements to the sun. While nothing is proven by this intuition in the natural man, no proof is needed, none sought. That the intuition persists is justification enough for following it.

The insistence on proof is a modern obsession at any rate. It was not pursued as a requisite for belief before the so-called Age of Enlightenment. In the soul of man there is a capacity to live by a range of experience and wisdom that transcends his own analysis and upon which he can validly manage his present, plan his future, and construct a civilization. Religious response to the question of life and death has always been part of that capacity. It is upon this fact that all God's revelation works, stage by stage, to bring humanity to the knowledge and love of the Father through the Son in the Holy Spirit.

And that is why the Bible abounds in images of light. It is because of man's receptivity to that which he does not always understand. It is also because there has ever been, alongside this receptivity, a darkness of spirit of one kind or another in the human soul crying out for reassurance. To this cry the inspired word offers consolation by drawing creatively upon the natural source of his hope, the blessed light of day, and making it a supernatural symbol of the beatific light that dispels eternal darkness. Indeed the doubt, desperation and despair provide the perfect backdrop for such images. Even the black night of the soul contributes to the saving plan of the revealing God who makes use of all that happens to make himself known. Witness the Book of Qoheleth for instance: the Preacher of the vanity of all human endeavour whose holy pessimism rivals even the grimmest philosophical existentialism of our own time, yet whose honesty about life before Christ only enhances the splendour of the New Testament message.

Anticipating that splendour in the Old Testament, and celebrating its arrival in the New, scripture glistens with references to the bright fires of dawn, the sun's coming up like a bridegroom from his tent, its high flares at noon, its intensity even while descending, its gentle glow at evening. By way of contrast we have also the mists and the darkness, the terror of night, the impenetrable cloud, the density of storm. From the very beginning however it is made clear that God separated the light from the dark. His first creative act was to subdue the 'darkness on the face of the deep' (Gen. 1:2). 'And God said, "Let there be light"; and there was light. And God saw that the light

was good; and God separated the light from the darkness'
(Gen. 1:3–4). On the fourth day, to ensure a supremacy of
brightness, he 'made the two great lights, the greater light to
rule the day, and the lesser light to rule the night; he made
the stars also' (Gen. 1:16). Allowing for the sixth century
BC cosmological world view, which distinguished between
daylight and sunlight without connecting the two, it is interesting (and amusing) to read this account as a Hebrew satire
on Babylonian astrology and solar deities. Elohim alone
is God Most High. The sun which other nations worship,
he neglected to make until well into the week of creation!
Only the foolish (that is, the hated Chaldean enemy) who
did not know the true God – the God of Israel – would
deify a star!

The primacy of light in God's list of priorities, and its
firm and permanent distinction from the dark as laid
down by the Genesis myth was to set the course of an
important theological theme through the rest of the Bible.
That although night and day vie with one another till the
end of time, the void and the darkness can never defeat the
light because the light is the created image of God himself.
It is life. John's Gospel – the Genesis of the New Testament – articulates the meaning of the metaphor with
unambiguous doctrinal clarity: 'In the beginning ... the
Word was God ... (and) all things were made through
him ... In him was life, and the life was the light of men.
The light shines in the darkness, and the darkness has not
overcome it' (1:1–4).

Because Jesus is light from light, splendour of the Father's
glory, true God from true God, his triumph as Sol Invictus
is God's own pre-eminence over all the spiritual forces of
his creation. This is why St Paul assures the Colossians of
Christ's victory over 'the elemental spirits of the universe
(now that he has) disarmed the principalities and powers,
triumphing over them' (Col. 2:8; 15), a point he repeats in
his letter to the Ephesians: '(Christ sits) above all rule and
authority and power and dominion, and above every name
that is named, not only in this age but also in that which is to
come' (1:21). In both instances he attributes Jesus' glorious
supremacy to his resurrection from the dead (Col. 2:12–13;
Eph. 1:20).

But how does scripture mean us to understand the image of light which the New Testament links with Easter, an event which the Old Testament could barely have imagined, and which even we can scarcely grasp today? What precisely is the Church praying for on December 21st when it calls on the Rising Sun to come and enlighten those who sit in darkness and in death's shadow? In a word it is Justice. 'O Rising Sun, you are ... the sun of justice'.

For Isaiah, justice meant rescuing God's people in Galilee from constant foreign oppression. Galilee, situated in the north of Palestine, was early prey to every invading marauder descending by way of the Fertile Crescent. Flanked by the sea, it was exposed to maritime attack as well. 'Galilee of the nations', Isaiah termed it sympathetically; 'Way of the sea'; 'Land beyond (the security of) the Jordan' (9:1). This vulnerable and isolated province had reason more than most to be gloomy and anguished. When waves of invaders swept down from the northlands in the eighth century BC it was utterly submerged in the deluge. With reassuring alacrity equal to the need Isaiah invoked the justice of God and promised a deliverance as certain as the dawn. 'There will be no gloom for her that was in anguish ... The people who walked in darkness have seen a great light; those who dwelt in a land of deep darkness, on them has light shined' (9:1−2). Still writing during the crisis, he uses the past tense as if their deliverance had already come. It is technically called the 'prophetic perfect' − the device by which the absolute certitude of God's future is established. It could not be otherwise, for God is the God of the covenant. He has sworn by his own self to stand by his people. His divine righteousness demands of him that he act on their behalf, never abandoning them to a situation that is not right. Isaiah therefore dares to speak of joy. 'You have increased the joy (of) the nation; they rejoice before you as with joy at the harvest, as men rejoice when they divide the spoil' (9:3). Already the yoke is (as good as) lifted from the shoulder, every trampling boot and blood-drenched garment burned, the tumult of warfare ended. This nation will survive, will rise again.

As the guarantee of divine rectification, the Galileans can expect the appearance of an ideal king who will set matters to right in an ideal way. Again the prophet speaks as if this had already happened. 'For to us a child is born, to us a son is given; and the government will be upon his shoulder, and his name will be called "Wonderful Counsellor, Mighty God, Everlasting Father, Prince of Peace" ... Of the increase of his government and of peace there will be no end ... with justice and righteousness from this time forth' (9:6—7). This passage constitutes the first reading of the Midnight Mass at Christmas and provides the Introit for the liturgy on Christmas morning. Thus the Church regards Christ's nativity as the fulfilment of God's pledge to bring justice where justice is needed. This has always been the tradition since Christmas was first celebrated back in the fourth century. The liturgy takes its cue from St Matthew who saw in Jesus' ministry around the towns of Galilee the literal accomplishment of Isaiah's promise which he cites in his Gospel at length (4:12—16).

Of course Matthew's perception of justice was different from Isaiah's. For one thing the political situation had changed. For another, the gospel is not about political idealism. The light which it proclaims is of a different order, one that transcends every form of government and spans all systems of social organization. In fact through the course of scripture the idea of justice underwent a great deal of development in accord with the experiences of God's people and the understanding of their writers. This is why there is no single word in biblical Hebrew that precisely matches our concept of justice. Their language has a rich variety of terms to cover all that the concept implies. But common to each of these was the notion of putting right something that was wrong. Moreover, that God alone was the supreme administrator of justice since man was not always to be trusted, and indeed not always capable of rectifying his mistakes. At every stage of the Bible's exploration of the matter, the symbolism of light proved extremely apt. It enabled the Hebrews to grasp that all forms of injustice belonged to the same gathering darkness that overshadows the human condition, curtailing man's progress. It also affirmed their belief that, by dint of his luminous nature, God abhors unrighteousness at whatever level it occurs and to whatever degree.

Consequently in the Old and New Testaments it is always the 'anawim — the poor of YHWH — who most deserved

God's protection. They were the truly vulnerable in society —
the stranger, the widow and the orphan (to quote scripture's
classic turn of phrase) — because they had no voice of their
own. Therefore they looked to God himself for the redress
of their grievances since no one else would take their part.
These are the ones Jesus called the poor in spirit, whom
he placed first on his list of the blessed of his Father's
kingdom. They were the first Advent community. All their
hope was exercised in waiting for God to come and intervene
in their cause. For their sake would the ideal king be sent and
anointed. He would take in hand their needs, would personally undertake the requirements of their right to justice. As
a result this figure, like the image of light and the theme of
justice itself, turns up consistently in many forms through
the books of Hebrew scripture.

He was there before Isaiah and continued to appear after
him. He personified rectitude. In two senses. Not only would
he rectify the wrongs of the oppressed, but in the precise religious sense of the word he would establish moral uprightness,
righteousness, correct living. His kingdom would be a State
of proper, decent values where righteousness would be at
home, that is, would be the norm. He is the subject of many
of the psalms. Ps.71/72 for instance. Here he is presented as
commanding the respect and allegiance not simply of all in
Israel, but of all nations.

> O God, give your judgment to the king,
> to a king's son your justice,
> that he may judge your people in justice
> and your poor in right judgment.
>
> May he defend the poor of the people
> and save the children of the needy
> and crush the oppressor.
>
> In his days justice shall flourish
> and peace till the moon fails.
> Before him all kings shall fall prostrate,
> all nations shall serve him.
>
> For he shall save the poor when they cry
> and the needy who are helpless.

He will have pity on the weak
and save the lives of the poor.
From oppression he will rescue their lives,
to him their blood is dear.

As a mark of his perfect commitment and the everlasting quality of his accomplishment, he himself is compared to the light.

He shall endure like the sun and the moon
from age to age.
May his name be blessed for ever
and endure like the sun.

In Deutero- and Trito-Isaiah he merges into the figure of God himself. The metaphor now explodes in a dazzling epiphany of breath-catching brightness.

Arise, shine; for your light has come, and the glory of the Lord has risen upon you. For behold darkness shall cover the earth, and thick darkness the peoples; but the Lord will arise upon you, and his glory will be seen upon you. And nations shall come to your light, and kings to your dawning brightness . . .
The sun shall no more be your light by day, nor for brightness shall the moon give light to you by night; but the Lord will be your everlasting light, and your God will be your glory. Your sun shall no more go down, nor your moon withdraw itself; for the Lord will be your everlasting light, and your days of mourning shall be ended (Is. 60:1–3; 19–20).

I will lead the blind in a way that they know not; in paths that they have not known I will guide them. I will turn the darkness before them into light (Is. 42:10–16).

The Isaian school did not intend a strict identification of the ideal king with God himself. The messianic bearer of light would be God's envoy, not YHWH in person. But the sun motif did permit the prophetic tradition to link the two very closely indeed. God and his messenger, glory from the

Glory, justice from the source of Justice, one the instrument of the other, completing the task on earth that radiated from heaven. The intimate association of all these ideas — God, his justice, his king, the light — was not new, nor was it exclusive to Israelite religious thought. A thousand years before First Isaiah the Akkadian solar deity, Shamash, was worshipped as a god of justice. The king of this Old Babylonian, Amorite dynasty on the banks of the Euphrates, was said to have received the sun-god's blessing on a moral inventory that comprised 282 laws — five centuries before Moses received the commandments from YHWH on Mount Sinai. Known as the Code of Hammurabi, after the young monarch who inscribed it, this gift from the sun was testimony to his god's solicitude for the ethical welfare of this civilization in justice and peace. Although the dynasty declined like a stella nova after only two and a half centuries, its cultural brilliance was a veritable sun-burst whose radiance influenced Babylonian civilization — and ultimately Hebrew thought too — for a great time after.

While Isaiah of course never confused the celebration of justice with solar apotheosis, his expression of Israel's hope in the language of the dawning light would have been perfectly in keeping with contemporary Middle Eastern thought processes. Even Jesus, describing the indiscriminate generosity of the Father's merciful justice, depicted his meaning in this way. 'Love your enemies and pray for those who persecute you, so that you may be sons of your Father who is in heaven; for he makes his sun rise on the evil and on the good' (Matt. 5:44–45). What is significant about Isaiah's use of the sun-justice imagery alongside his preoccupation with the ideal king, is this: it provided a convenient vocabulary for the New Testament later to present Jesus as the literal fulfilment of every possible implication of Semitic and non-Semitic light-and-justice symbolism. In Christ is to be found not only God's right judgement, his enlightening teaching, his ideal government, his sound justice, his promised messiah — but in fact the divine nature, God himself.

All the Old Testament prophets including Isaiah saw a direct connection between political disruption and moral disorder. Injustice was both cause and effect of Israel's problems. Social upheavals accompanied social exploitation; national calamities were the manifestation of the nation's disregard for the law. To redress the imbalance of social or political chaos therefore, a change of heart had to take place in the moral sphere. But this did not happen often, and it never lasted long. Even after the catastrophes of the eighth and sixth centuries the problematic darkness prevailed from Dan to Beersheba. Despite the lessons that should have been learned, human stubbornness still preferred night to day. The post-exilic prophets watched with dismay the old errors recurring. Personal immorality, public and private; social corruption; marital breakdown through infidelity and divorce; empty forms of worship; polluted sacrifices and external ritual without interior commitment to the Lord. Worst of all, by the time of Malachi − one of the last of the prophetic line − it seemed that the unjust and the wicked actually thrived while the oppressed and the poor looked on! Why did God stand aside and let the evil prosper, the righteous asked? What was the point of doing right if God did not even take notice?

It was against the louring sky of this bleak background that Malachi addressed the cheerless and discouraged faithful of YHWH with a word of memorable consolation. It was to be the last time a hallowed and familiar image would be used by a prophet, for the age of the prophets was drawing to a close.

For you who fear my name the sun of righteousness will rise, with healing in its wings. You shall go forth leaping like calves from the stall. And you shall tread down the wicked, for they will be ashes under the soles of your feet, on the day when I act, says the Lord of hosts (4:2−3).

This delightful rural cameo, catching the freshness at the start of a new day and the vitality of young cattle going out to pasture, vibrant and energetic in the morning sunlight, conveys the exuberance of a prophet's vision, of a poet's insight. The orient sun will bring healing to the rifts and schisms of God's people. It is not merely a renewal of political life that is intended here, nor the restoration of social welfare, although these are not necessarily excluded. It is primarily a spiritual renewal that the context suggests. A salving of the root cause of all injustice: the diseased and malignant inner man which cannot grow strong because it has been confined so long in the dark. When the morning rises, as the prophet swears it will, then those who hunger and thirst for righteousness will be satisfied, will no longer mourn the dominance of evil, nor have to endure persecution for justice' sake. They shall have the earth for their heritage. Theirs will be the kingdom of heaven.

Thus at the very sunset of prophecy, a dawning is predicted whose lustrous rays will usher in the messianic era. A new creation is soon to begin. Prophecy, having fulfilled its purpose, declines gracefully, flushed with vermilion promise of the greater light that is to come.

With the infancy narrative of the Gospel according to Luke that light bursts forth out of the winter darkness as splendidly as an Arctic sunrise. It is all and more that the seers promised. Each incident of the first two chapters is a different colour, one more stunning than the last. Together they form a magnificent kaleidoscope of bright shapes that rotate like sun-flares around the figure of the Infant Christ. The language of the text is suffused with images of cosmic light. The lasting impression is one of darkness utterly dispelled in an aurora never imagined since Eden. St Luke recounts its beauty to his most excellent Theophilus with all the enthusiasm of a shepherd blowing his horn after a dark and stormy night.

The birth of Jesus is signalled by a sudden explosion of brightness in the nightskies over Bethlehem. A midnight aurora borealis illuminates the fields around the Judean village startling the shepherds who keep the long night vigil with their sheep. 'In that region there were shepherds out in the field, keeping watch over their flock by night. And an angel of the Lord appeared to them, and the glory of the Lord shone around them, and they were filled with fear. And the angel said to them, "Be not afraid; for behold, I bring you good news of a great joy which will come to all the people; for to you is born this day in the city of David a Saviour, who is Christ the Lord"' (2:8 – 10).

The event is enclosed before and after with two great canticles of light: the Benedictus intoned by Zechariah, and Simeon's Nunc Dimittis whose joyful strains resound through the chambers of the Temple in Jerusalem.

With the first of these the father of John the Baptist finds voice to bless the Lord God of Israel who has visited his people in person to redeem them. Earlier struck dumb through his lack of belief he symbolizes all those in Israel who doubted the God of justice. Now he also stands for those who recognize and accept that God has finally 'raised up a mighty saviour . . . as he promised by the lips of . . . those who were his prophets from of old' (Luke 1:69–70). Fulfilling the oath made to Abraham, the covenant with Moses, the assurance of prophecy, this Saviour will ensure that 'free from fear, and saved from the hands of our foes we (will) serve (God) in holiness and justice all the days of our life' (1:71–75). The Baptist is to be his forerunner.

As for you, little child,
you shall be called a prophet of God, the Most High.
You shall go ahead of the Lord
to prepare his ways before him,
To make known to his people their salvation
through forgiveness of all their sins,
the loving-kindness of the heart of our God
who visits us like the dawn from on high.
He will give light to those who sit in darkness,
those who dwell in the shadow of death,
and guide us into the way of peace (1:76–79).

It is from this canticle that the 'O' antiphon of December 21st is taken in full. Here are combined all the themes of hope initiated in the Old Testament and completed by the appearance of Jesus. The justice, which Jewish political history and Israel's moral failure taught men to long for, is now revealed as salvation. St Luke uses the term or its derivatives no less than six times throughout this prologue to the Gospel. It is synonymous with mercy, forgiveness, loving-kindness. It is a justifying justice that God has had in mind from the beginning. Not even the prophets could have guessed how radiant a morning they had forecast.

The darkness theme is also explained. It is not simply misfortune or suffering or life's disappointments. It is the

'shadow of death' – physical and spiritual – which the
Letter to the Hebrews says held men in the bondage of
fear all their life (2:15) but from which all are now made
free by Christ's destruction of the one 'who has the power
of death, that is, the devil' (2:14).

The entire range and use of the symbols of light is shown
to be more than just imagery. The simile has merged into
reality. The Son of God is himself the Sun of Justice. His
very appearing effects the healing required among the sons
of men. His presence makes God present. His incarnation
brings a new form of life on earth; a new way of living;
a new way of dying. Human nature is changed in the way
plant-life is changed as winter turns to spring. The moral
climate has shifted. The fog and mist of our incapacity to
please God has been pierced by the powerful first rays of
dawning grace. Truly, the Benedictus is a morning hymn
of praise uttered by a new generation, a new race out
of Eden.

In the second canticle the range and effect of the Rising
Sun are universalized. The tired eyes of the ancient Simeon
see what from ancient times Israel longed to see but never
saw. They see even more: a sunrise that will colour the skies
of every people to the ends of the earth.

> At last, all powerful Master,
> you give leave to your servant to go in peace,
> according to your promise.
> For my eyes have seen your salvation
> which you have prepared for all nations,
> the light to enlighten the Gentiles
> and give glory to Israel, your people (2:29–32).

For this old man the words of the Benedictus have already
come true. He is no longer afraid of approaching death.
Holding the child of Mary in his arms, he holds Life itself.
With the wisdom of faith and a life-time of waiting in hope
he embodies the peace that Christian death brings to those
who have seen God's word realize itself, who have embraced
salvation in their mind and heart as one embraces a new-
born child. No longer held captive by the fear of death
nor seated in its paralysing shadow of darkness, he speaks

the thanks of all who, even in old age, experience the rejuvenating breath of the Spirit of the Risen Sun. Truly, the Nunc Dimittis is a hymn for the blessed night-time which no longer threatens the Day, whose spiritual radiance never sets.

Zechariah and Simeon – and Elizabeth and Anna, daughter of Phanuel – all of them elderly players in the first act of Luke's drama of salvation. They are deliberately chosen to bridge the Old and New Testaments. They represent the ancient 'anawim, YHWH's faithful dependants, bowed with the expectations of a Hebrew millennium. Like the lamp of prophecy which shone in a dark place until the morning star should arise (2 Pet. 1:19), and like the (passing) gleam of the Law which once comforted a people in waiting (2 Cor. 3:7–11), these venerable characters enact the point of the old dispensation. They show its preparatory function in the waiting for Christ, bear witness to the truth that the law and the prophets, faithfully followed, are not an end in themselves but lead to the redeeming justice of Jesus. Their canticles, incorporated by the Church into the Liturgy of the Hours, by which daily time is sanctified through prayer, are a permanent feature of divine worship at the start and the end of each day. At Lauds and at Compline they echo the most repeated refrain in scripture, one that combines the aspirations for holiness before Christ with the gratitude of the grace after Christ: 'From the rising of the sun to its setting, praised be the name of the Lord.'

The object of this praise is the resurrection. In Jesus' rising from the dead is recognized the pledge of resurrection for all. His achievement is the ultimate restoration of justice, in the sense that mortality was not part of the Creator's plan. Not part of his sense of what is right. Death is an anomaly in the arena of his handiwork. Cemeteries are an abhorrence to the God of Life.

Death was never of God's fashioning; not for his pleasure does life cease to be; what meant his creation, but that all created things should have being? No breed has he created on earth but for its thriving; none carries within itself the seeds of its own destruction. Think not that mortality bears sway on earth; no end nor term is fixed to a life well lived (Wisd. of Sol. 1:13 – 15. KNOX).

Where did death come from then if not from God? According to the Book of Wisdom it came from man's unrighteousness. Sin introduced into the world an element that was alien to it, a thing unthinkable to the mind of God. This too was an injustice – the ingratitude of the race in whom the Lord had stamped the seal of his Being. One injustice bred the other, and a golden thread was broken.

Written (probably) in the last century BC, this work went further than any previous text in affirming clearly and categorically a future life after death: it would consist of a really different existence in God's presence for the just. But it stopped short of promising bodily resurrection. Hebrew scripture did not seriously consider such a thing until very late. Where the language of resurrection is used it mostly refers to the survival of Israel as a nation and not of individuals, except in the sense of genealogical survival through one's children (which is not resurrection at all). In the handful of cases where it is more strongly asserted (Dan. 12:2, for example), it cannot be taken as representative of pre-Christian biblical theology. Hence there was never a faith-consensus about resurrection and it never became part of received Jewish doctrine. It was nevertheless a subject of popular debate so that by Jesus' time the Pharisees and Sadducees were divided over the matter.

It was for St Paul – with his Pharisaic background, his intimate knowledge of the Book of Wisdom, and his familiarity with Platonic dualism as well as Jewish thought processes – to formulate a Christian soteriology based on the fact of Jesus' rising from the tomb. Accepting Wisdom's premise that death insinuated its way into man's life through sin, he demonstrates how deliverance from death is accomplished by Christ's victory over iniquity.

As sin came into the world through one man and death through sin ... (so) by a man has come also the resurrection of the dead. For as in Adam all die, so also in Christ shall all be made alive (Rom. 5:12; 1 Cor. 15:21 – 22).

Contemporary Pauline studies have drawn attention to the Apostle's emphasis on Easter as essential to the mystery of redemption. It is the necessary complement of the crucifixion, for while the cross pays for the sin of the world, the resurrection vindicates that payment, confirms its receipt and cancels the debt. Without an Easter rising, Good Friday would have been pointless.

> If Christ has not been raised, your faith is futile and you are still in your sins. Then those also who have fallen asleep in Christ have perished. If for this life only we have hoped in Christ, we are of all men most to be pitied.
> But in fact Christ has been raised from the dead, the first fruits of those who have fallen asleep (1 Cor. 15:17−20).

In the light of the Paschal Mystery our rising from the grave is an absolute certainty. For Paul it is a simple matter of justice, and he argues it as such. God could not exclude any son of Adam from eternal life who has been baptized into Christ's death because the one who died was the innocent Son of God. As the Father delivered Jesus from the depths of the tomb, so in justice he is obliged to raise up also those who are Christ's body. Man's justification before God is his faith in the resurrection. We will not have to justify ourselves any further at the seat of judgement: Christ alone is justification enough for each and for all.

> If you confess with your lips that Jesus is Lord and believe in your heart that God raised him from the dead, you will be saved ...
> If Christ is in you, although your bodies are dead because of sin, your spirits are alive because of righteousness. If the Spirit of him who raised Jesus from the dead dwells in you, he who raised Christ Jesus from the dead will give life to your mortal bodies also through his Spirit who dwells in you (Rom. 10:9; 8:10−11).

At the time Paul was composing these texts (AD 57−58), elaborating the theology of resurrection in doctrinal terms, the Gospel narratives of the Easter event were still at the oral stage of transmission. When they came to be written down they synthesized all the complex implications of such faith-reflection in their simple account of the discovery of the empty tomb. The meaning was in part conveyed by the timing of the discovery – a point on which all the evangelists concur. It was a dawning experience. In the Johannine tradition the stone had been taken away 'while it was still dark' (20:1). According to Matthew the women arrived at the scene 'toward the dawn' (28:1). Luke chronicles their find 'at early dawn' (24:1), while for Mark the moment is 'very early . . . when the sun had risen' (16:2; cf. 16:9 of the Marcan Appendix). Read in this sequence, the verbal pictures of the apostolic tradition, like the frames of a film in slow motion, form a contemplative study of the Paschal Sunrise. The passover from dark to light, from night to morning, from death to life. The effect is more vivid, because more imaginative, than any straightforward narrative could achieve. It conveys an extraordinary sense of what happened to Jesus, yet without disturbing the mystery of it all.

The unanimity of the Gospels on the timing undoubtedly reflects the historical fact of the matter. But may we not discern in the emphasis of that fact a significance beyond chronological interest? The evangelists were well aware of the sunrise prophecies of Malachi, First and Second Isaiah, the Psalms, as well as the light-and-justice imagery in the Old Testament from Genesis onward. Sensitive as they were in their own writings to the nuance of words, the emotive effect of language, is not safe to assume that they deliberately synchronized Jesus' rising with the rising of the new day, the Day of the Lord? For them, as for Paul, this was not simply the start of a new chapter of history. It was the transformation of history itself, of the world, of all creation, and most especially of human destiny.

And so we end where we began: with the rays of a rising sun illuminating an ancient burial chamber. Not the pallid light of a pre-Celtic winter, caught by some shrewdly aligned Megalithic cairn still full of bones. But the vigorous warmth of a spring dawn, rising on the broken seal of an empty tomb in Palestine. These rays shine upon a stone that has been rolled back forever. They invade an inner darkness which — like the spirit of man — lies joyfully open to the graced brightness of eternal life.

Like the first disciples running to that empty tomb on Easter morning, who 'saw and believed' (John 20:8), the Church too knows how to gaze in at bright emptiness and discern there a fullness of meaning. Such a faith as this lightens the vacancy of winter-waiting, and enjoins a community to celebrate with thanks and praise the December birth of its Easter Saviour.

Chapter Seven

O King of Nations

December 22nd. O King whom all the peoples desire, you are the cornerstone which makes all one. O come and save man whom you made from clay.

At the beginning and end of Jesus' ministry scripture represents or records the presence and witness of the nations. The Gospel opens with wise men from the East coming to Jerusalem in search of him who is born King of the Jews (Matt. 2:1–2). Just before the Passion, according to John, there came to that same city some Greeks who said to Philip, 'Sir, we wish to see Jesus' (12:21). At Calvary the inscription above the cross was written in three languages – Hebrew, Latin and Greek.

At the beginning and end of the Church's ministry the New Testament notes the same phenomenon. On the day of Pentecost, start of the universal mission from Jerusalem, devout men 'from every nation under heaven' heard and understood the first preaching of the gospel (Acts 2:5). When that task is fulfilled, says the Apocalypse, the new Jerusalem will host a hundred and forty-four thousand. Twelve times twelve thousand – the number of completeness, 'a great multitude ... from every nation, from all tribes and peoples and tongues' (7:4,9). 'O King whom all the peoples desire ... come and save man', prays the Church in the time in between.

There has always been a great desire for Christ, a great need. 'The gospel is bringing blessings and spreading through the whole world, just as it has among you', St Paul told the Colossians (1:16. TEV). As in Paul's time, so also now. What Christ has to offer is very attractive: unity among peoples.

Real unity, born out of peace with God, developing into multi-national fraternity, but beginning as integrity on the level of the individual person. It is the dream of civilisation. Not one achieved so far, however, by the advances in science and technology, politics and art. For all that is good in these areas, the dream is still no more than an elusive reality. Indeed it is doubtful whether civilization really understands the nature of the peace it is seeking. And yet the enthusiasm for goodwill that Christmas generates year by year, for reconciliation, for laying down arms, suggests a tacit acknowledgement that lasting harmony is related ultimately to the Kingship of Christ.

The best that diplomacy can ever achieve is the uneasy truce, a temporary cessation of violence, a precarious equilibrium between conflict and concord. This best is never enough. Those who negotiate know well, as Vatican 11 put it, that 'peace is not merely the absence of war. Nor can it be reduced solely to the maintenance of a balance of power between opposing forces' (GS, §78). Given that history is strewn with the shards of broken agreements and the debris of aggression, what is amazing is not the recurrence of conflict but that peace should still be regarded as an attainable ideal. For it is a fact that the initiative for international order and cooperation has never been pursued on so grand a scale as now.

That spirit of conciliation, more vigorous and determined than its counterpart and just as persistent, is the spirit of the incarnation. It signals the presence in history of the Prince of Peace whose reign has already begun and will not cease until its purpose is achieved. Each year on December 22nd the voice of the Church harmonizes with the spirit of all mankind in a common aspiration for a better future. The Advent title of that day is indeed more than an aspiration. It is a prophecy. Not only does it summon to a new world order; it actually establishes what it proclaims. By calling the nations to faith in the 'cornerstone which makes all one' it is, by that action, laying the basis of a better society. By announcing a Kingdom built on rock, it declares unstable all sites on sand. For the men of clay there is a new foundation upon which their noble efforts for peace, once re-located, will be saved from collapse. Jesus, the antiphon seems to say, is the joy of man's desiring precisely because his act of redemption puts communion among men within reach as a present possibility, not just an eschatological hope. Because of the Nativity, world peace is no romantic day-dream. It is an inevitability.

The idea of the cornerstone upon which God builds a strong and united people is a favourite and recurring one in the Old and New Testaments equally. Drawn from the prodigious building programme that continued throughout Israel long after the Settlement, its relevance would have been obvious to town or city dwellers and country folk alike. The function of the stone placed at the corner was to integrate two walls running in different directions. The north-south wall and the east-west one, no longer at odds with each other, were now bonded together to secure the building and give it lasting solidity. Thus two contraries were made to cooperate for the good of the whole, bringing to the work a marvellous strength through their very differences. Nowhere was this metaphor so apt than with reference to the Temple. Here the hand of man and the mind of God laboured together, constructing, rebuilding, extending, improving the grandest edifice in Judah which took centuries to complete and stood for the nation itself that hailed God as its King. Like the Temple that nation was integrated in all its tribal diversity, North, South, East, West, insofar as there was common convergence on the cultic sacrifice of the old Covenant.

For Paul of Tarsus the true cornerstone of God, however, was not the one in the Jewish Temple, but Jesus.

He is our peace, who has made us (Jew- and Gentile-Christians) both one, and has broken down the dividing wall of hostility ... that he might create in himself one new man in place of the two, so making peace, and might reconcile us both to God in one body through the cross, thereby bringing the hostility to an end ... So then you are ... fellow citizens with the saints and members of the household of God, built upon the foundation of the apostles and prophets, Christ Jesus himself being the cornerstone, in whom the whole structure is joined together and grows into a holy temple in the Lord; in

whom you also are built into it for a dwelling place of
God in the Spirit (Eph. 2:14–22).

One notices here a certain twist in the image which it never
had in the Old Testament. A dividing wall has been demolished. The cornerstone is that of another structure, different
from – though somehow related to – what stood there
before. Whether this passage was written by Paul himself
before the destruction of the Temple in Jerusalem by the
Romans in AD 70, or by one of Paul's disciples shortly
after the event, is a debate that goes on apace and need not
concern us here. What is certain is that for the Apostle the
Jerusalem Temple became redundant in the wake of what
God did for his people in Christ. New Testament writers
after AD 70, who were aware for sure of what the Romans
had done, agreed with Paul. The Book of the Apocalypse
depicts the heavenly Jerusalem without a temple. It was no
longer necessary among the communion of saints. Their
unity was assured by the presence of the Lamb. 'I saw
no temple in the city, for its temple is the Lord God
Almighty and the Lamb ... By its light shall the nations
walk; and the kings of the earth shall bring their glory into
it' (21:22–24).

The dividing wall that Paul speaks of, torn down theologically by the power of the cross, was that which separated the
Court of the Gentiles (located around the perimeter of the
Temple precincts) from the Court of the Women. Although
just five feet high – easy enough to jump over – it was an
unsuperable barrier between Jewish and Gentile nations. To
cross over it meant certain death for the stranger. In 1871
archaeologists unearthed three marble plaques that once
adorned the wall with the threat of capital punishment.
They were inscribed in all the principal languages of the
time. Their legend ran: 'Let no one of any other nation
come within the fence and barrier around the Holy Place.
Whosoever will be taken doing so will himself be respon-
sible for the fact that his death will ensue.' Both in tone and
in purpose it was the epitome of hostility.

What the crucified Christ tore down was the hostility that
the barrier represented. He did away in fact with the whole
Jewish system of law and punishment, ritual and sacrifice

that the Temple enshrined. His God would no longer be confined in a Holy of Holies, a darkened, windowless inner Sanctum around which the world remained divided. That secret place was now thrown open to the lives of all. God was exposed to the nations in his Son on Calvary. His blood would wash away the fear of man for man, and the fear of men for God.

St Luke, Paul's travel companion, stressed the same idea in his portrayal of Jesus' death. 'It was now about the sixth hour, and there was darkness over the whole land until the ninth hour, while the sun's light failed; and the curtain of the temple was torn in two. Then Jesus, crying with a loud voice, said, "Father, into thy hands I commit my spirit!" And having said this he breathed his last' (23:44 – 46). The curtain was that which shrouded the Holiest Place from view. The earthquake of Good Friday had buckled the massive pillars that supported the curtain-rail. Each falling in the opposite direction, they caused the veil to be rent down the middle. Jesus was dead and the days of the Temple worship were over. A new covenant had been cut that would embrace all men in a single family consecrated to the Father by the perfect sacrifice of the Son. It was a theme that the Letter to the Hebrews would take up and develop later in the century, long after Paul's death and perhaps Luke's too.

After the spiritual seismic eruption of Calvary, whose historical after-shock four decades later resulted in the complete physical collapse of the Temple, the work of reconstruction had to begin. It was not to be as it was before. The visible sanctuary of God's presence was never replaced. But the divine Masterbuilder was already busy at his trade. Recalling an ancient text from Isaiah that called Israel to a totally trusting dependence on God, the writer of First Peter found the ideal mode of explaining to his newly-baptised congregation the blue-print of God's new dwelling place on earth:

'Behold, I am laying in Zion a stone, a cornerstone chosen and precious, and he who believes in him will not be put to shame'.

To you therefore who believe he is precious, but for those who do not believe, 'The very stone which the builders rejected has become the head of the corner' (1 Pet. 2:6–7, incorporating Is. 28:16 and Ps. 118:22).

The original context of the Isaiah quotation was Judah's political terror in the face of the Assyrian threat to their national territory. Would they yield to their fear by seeking protection through an unwise alliance with Egypt? Or would they choose YHWH as their King and rely on his power to save? Believe in the Lord, advised the prophet, and rest your weight upon him. He alone is a rock to lean on.

So often during that crisis and the ones that followed the Israelites made the wrong choice. They rejected the summons to faith. In New Testament times they even rejected Jesus himself. Yet in God's architectural plan he was the very keystone of man's future peace and security. Echoing the urgency of Isaiah, the author of First Peter admonishes the new community not to repeat the mistakes of their spiritual ancestors:

> Come to him, to that living stone, rejected by men but in God's sight chosen and precious; and like living stones be yourselves built into a spiritual house, to be a holy priesthood, to offer spiritual sacrifices acceptable to God through Jesus Christ ... (For) you are a chosen race, a royal priesthood, a holy nation, God's own people (2:4–5; 9).

Suddenly all that was obscure becomes clear. What had been deemed a calamity on the Mount of Zion – the death of Christ, the demolition of the Temple – is no calamity at all. It is the start of the glorious age of the Kingdom. Henceforth God's dwelling-place is not just among men, but within them. The cessation of blood-sacrifices is no cause for lament: God's justice is eternally satisfied in the offering of his Son. The end of Levitical priesthood is a great blessing: it marks the universal priesthood of the entire community. Every Christian act of love is now a sacrifice acceptable to the Father. The decline of Jerusalem as the lodestone of pilgrims is a reason to rejoice: now the pilgrims themselves are the sanctuary of the Holy One. They are a holy people, a royal priesthood. Accepting the Kingship of

Christ alone, they reign with him to whom they are subject and in whom they are one. The day has arrived that Jesus prophesied to the woman of Samaria. 'Believe me, the hour is coming when neither on this mountain nor in Jerusalem will you worship the Father ... The hour is coming, and now is, when the true worshippers will worship the Father in spirit and truth' (John 4:21, 23). Never again will the divine Presence be exclusively associated with a particular place. 'The Most High does not dwell in houses made with hands' (Acts 7:48). Through the incarnation of his Son and the extension of his Church, God's life will flood the universe and inundate the human race.

That life is unity and peace, the desire of nations.

The unity which the new Temple theme envisaged in the Apostolic period did not exclude diversity. On the contrary it thrived on it. Among the members of Christ's body who made up the living stones were many gifts, charisms and ministries. What brought them together in perfect unison was the one Spirit whom all shared. The Corinthian community was a particularly good example of a church enriched with all the spiritual graces: the utterance of wisdom, and of knowledge; faith; power for healing; miracles; prophecy; tongues, and the interpretation of tongues. The list of their ministries included apostles, prophets, teachers, miracle workers, healers, helpers, administrators and speakers. Yet in the lavish distribution of God's favours to them they were inseparably one at the Source of all grace.

> There are varieties of gifts, but the same Spirit; and there are varieties of service, but the same Lord; and there are varieties of working, but it is the same God who inspires them all in every one. To each is given the manifestation for the common good (1 Cor. 12:4−7. Cf. Rom. 12:6−8).

In regard to this the idea of the human body suggested itself as an ideal working model of the kind of temple Paul had in mind. 'Just as the body is one and has many members, and all the members of the body, though many, are one body, so it is with Christ ... Now you are the body of Christ and individually members of it' (1 Cor. 12:12; 27. Cf. Rom. 12:4−5; Eph. 4:11−12). The living body, the living temple − the two ideas were interchangeable, equally important. One was not relinquished at the expense of the other. In his advice to the Corinthians on sexual matters, Paul found the perfect opportunity for mixing his metaphors: 'Do you not know that your bodies are members of Christ? ... that your body is a temple of the Holy Spirit within you, which you have from God? So glorify God in your body' (1 Cor. 6:15; 19−20).

For the most part however the dual imagery worked most successfully when applied to the entire community of a given church. There, where God was worshipped in the locale not of this city or that but in his spiritual abode, the ecclesial body of his Son (one Head and many members), there mankind could see for itself the grace and peace of the Lord Jesus Christ, the love of God and the fellowship of the Holy Spirit made visible in the lives of ordinary men and women. No distinction remained on the basis of Jew or Gentile, slave or freeman, male or female. There was no dividing wall to separate, no hostile plaque to exclude, no boundary defined by nationality, race or language. In a remarkable and unexpected way Isaiah's impossible dream had come to pass.

> It shall come to pass in the latter days that the mountain of the house of the Lord shall be established as the highest of the mountains ... and all the nations shall flow to it, and many peoples shall come and say: 'Come, let us go up to the mountain of the Lord, to the house of the God of Jacob; that he may teach us his ways and that we may walk in his paths ... He shall judge between the nations ... and they shall beat their swords into ploughshares, and their spears into pruning hooks; nation shall not lift up sword against nation, neither shall they learn war any more' (2:2−4).

It was the time anticipated by many an Israelite as he walked on the pilgrim route to the Holy City and, with tears in his eyes as its walls appeared, exchanged with his fellow traveller an ancient proverb, 'Thus says the Lord of hosts: In those days ten men from the nations of every tongue shall take a Jew by the sleeve and say, "We want to go with you, since we have learnt that God is with you"' (Zech. 8:23. JB).

Pruning hooks, ploughshares and pilgrimages. Not spears, swords and savagery. Agriculture instead of aggression, prayer in the place of imperialism. Did the dream ever really come true? For all the beauty of the language and the idealism of the prophets, the world is still smeared with blood, infected with segregation, sectarian to the core, gorged with arrogant nationalism, obese with the greed of exploitation and expansionism. Even St Paul's proclamation of the new age, the new creation, has not altered the fact that the belligerent instinct continues to dominate the affairs of world history with unabated and depressing consistency. Why, Corinth itself was riven with jealousy, quarrels, egotism, vanity and strife — all the symptoms of individualism that run contrary to the spirit of Christian freedom which preserves genuine oneness in the midst of legitimate pluralism.

It is with this sober picture in view and its feet firmly on cold ground that the Church in Advent implores Christ the Cornerstone to 'come and save man whom you made from clay'. In other words the temple is still under construction. The body of Christ has not yet grown up. The living stones are still earthy with grit. Their cement is not dry. The limbs of the organism lack strength. They are shot through with arthritic impediment. The Kingdom, if present in our midst, is not yet fully come. Each failure to unite reminds Christ's Church that it lives a continual Advent, that its prayer is a necessary part of the constant travail that St Paul said depicted the state of the whole of creation in the present age (Rom. 8:22). Paradoxically, the old and the new creation exist side by side, or perhaps one within the other. From whichever perspective, they appear alternately like a three-dimensional picture, sometimes even simultaneously. On closer inspection the new reality often seems to emerge through and as a result of the old disintegration. This is why the Church believes in salvation. It explains why it does not despair when its prayer seems to suffer a delay in response. What the community anticipates is an answer that actually comes via the struggle against evil. If there were no men of clay, no sin, no chaos, there would be no need of a cornerstone. To be in touch with that need is to know Christ and to experience the plan of redemption. It is to believe from the heart in the one whose first coming was 'to proclaim release to the captives, recovering of sight to the blind, to set at liberty those who are oppressed, to proclaim the acceptable year of the Lord' (Luke 4:18−19), and whose second coming will seal his purpose with success. In the meantime, the Kingdom is slowly, gradually, taking shape, but only at the cost of extended sacrifice.

The twin concepts of Church as body and temple are consolidated by the notion of sacrifice. The Temple was always the place where sacrifice was offered. The body is always the means by which the offering is rendered to God. In the new dispensation, because victim and priest are one and the same, the Church community itself is both the altar of the oblation for sin and the object of holocaust. In most of the texts of First Peter and the Pauline letters where the Church is considered as body-temple, the idea of sacrifice is never far away. 'You are a royal priesthood ... to offer spiritual sacrifices' (1 Pet. 2:9,5). 'I appeal to you, therefore, brethren ... to present your bodies as a living sacrifice, holy and acceptable to God, which is your spiritual worship' (Rom. 12:1).

The merit of such offerings is derived from the Church's mystical or sacramental communion with the Godhead. As body, it has Jesus for its head. As temple, it possesses him as cornerstone. As both, it has the Holy Spirit indwelling, whether as Soul within a living being or as Presence within a sanctuary. Consequently the sacrifice of the community is not different from, but part of the eternal sacrifice of the Son whose self-oblation on Calvary was inspired by and overshadowed by the Spirit. This is why the many spiritual sacrifices mentioned by First Peter are acceptable: it is Christ who has made them so by his integrating them into his own, who 'loved us and gave himself up for us, a fragrant offering and sacrifice to God' (Eph. 5:2).

The effect of such sacrifice is unity. Indeed there can be no unity without sacrifice. Even in the Old Testament, whose oblations foreshadowed the real thing, this was known.

> How good and how pleasant it is,
> when brothers live in unity!
> It is like precious oil upon the head
> running down upon the beard,
> running down upon Aaron's beard
> upon the collar of his robes (Ps. 132/133).

Here the cultic priesthood, symbolized by the bearded maturity of manhood and the holy anointing of Aaron, is equated with the unity of Israel. One is the effect of the other. Each is a source of great joy and rejoicing. The psalm is a celebration of the goodness of God who permits his people to draw close to him and one another through the mutual exchange of gifts. As with Noah after the flood, the burnt offering throughout Hebrew history marked the beginning of a new world, another covenant, an increase of the people, prosperity on the land, harmony among themselves.

Jesus' priesthood however was of a different order, as was his sacrifice at Golgotha. Therefore his Church's priestly ministry too is different from that of Aaron and the Levitical tradition. It is common human nature that the Father wishes to receive; ordinary men and women from whom he wishes to receive it. Common, in the sense that it belongs to all; human nature, insofar as it has been taken up by the Son of God into himself and sanctified. The Christian priesthood, the acceptable sacrifice, is nothing less than the human race joined inseparably to Christ who is himself consubstantially one with the Godhead. St Fulgentius of Ruspe, meditating on the in-depth treatment of this in the Letter to the Hebrews, understands salvation as nothing other than sacrificial communion:

> When mention is made of the priest, this refers to the mystery of the Lord's incarnation, whereby the Son of God ... 'though he was in the form of God, emptied himself, taking the form of a servant (becoming) obedient unto death' ...
> So, whilst remaining in the form of God, Christ is the only-begotten of God, to whom as to the Father we offer sacrifices; but by taking the form of a servant, Christ was

made priest through whom we can offer a living, holy sacrifice, pleasing to God. Nor could we have a sacrifice had not Christ become a victim for us; for in him the very nature of our race becomes a true and living sacrifice.
When we affirm that our prayers are offered through our Lord the eternal priest, we profess our faith that the true flesh of our race is in him ... (And) when we say 'your Son', and add: 'who lives and reigns with you in the unity of the Holy Spirit', we call to mind that unity which belongs to the nature of the Father and the Son and the Spirit: and we profess that it is one and the same Christ, one in nature with the Father and the Holy Spirit, who exercises the priestly office on our behalf (Epistle 14).

The priesthood of Christ resides in his humanity. In a different text than the one already cited, Fulgentius describes Jesus as 'true God and true priest' (*To Peter on Faith*, ch.22), thereby echoing the christological formula of Chalcedon − true God and true man − and so aligning the fleshly nature of the Son with his priestliness. By the same token the priesthood of the Church resides in its members' humanity. This is what it means to call it Christ's body. He has shared his incarnate capacity for sacrifice with his people just as he has shared with them his unity with the Father which, in his divine nature as God's Son, he never lost while on earth. And this is what it means to call the Church God's temple.

Unity, communion, *koinonia*, fellowship, sharing, oneness − all are new Testament terms that express the mystery of salvation. It was for this ideal that the Christ of the Fourth Gospel died willingly. 'That they may all be one. As you, Father, are in me and I am in you, may they also be in us ... That they may be one as we are one, I in them and you in me, that they may become completely one ... So that the love with which you have loved me may be in them, and I in them' (John 17:21; 23; 26). What is intended here is a complete participation in the perfect interplay of the three divine Persons of the Trinity who, while each remaining distinct and without confusion in their relationship with one another, nevertheless remain inseparably one so that we profess faith in a single God and not more. The concept of such a unity among men is a stunning one. Especially when we compare it with the divisions of the present time. Yet this is the Kingdom that Jesus, cornerstone and priest, came to proclaim and inaugurate. This is what he announced as 'already in your midst' and ratified by his crucifixion on Good Friday.

It is as the Crucified Christ that Jesus reigns over the dis-ordered world as its King. His suffering articulates the divisions among nations which are synonymous with evil. His agony exposes such evil for what it is by dramatizing its effects in his own human body. No one can look at the cross and remain indifferent to what those wounds are saying. For they also proclaim, by the Son of God's acceptance of them and his offering of them to his Father, the divine desire to heal them at their source and transform the human race into the wholesome and holy people it was created to be. That process begins by identifying evil in itself and differentiating it from the good. A difficult thing to do in any age, given man's distorted perception after original sin, but impossible without the truth of the cross.

If salvation is unification then sin is alienation. If communion is the nature of the highest good, not only its consequence but its essence, then disunity must be the essence of evil. The very word 'integrity', meaning virtuous, upright, righteous, also means whole, entire, undivided. Not only in itself but in relationship too. Disintegration on the other hand implies the end of the thing, a collapse in upon itself, no longer sustainable because no longer good. In every phase of existence the principle remains true: when anything is one it flourishes and there is harmony and peace. When it is divided it explodes with violent frustration and disturbs the tranquil balance of the cosmos.

Even the minutest particle of nature, the atom, once split causes nuclear destruction. Schizophrenia, the disease of the so-called split mind or personality, ruptures the normal life process in an unhappy human being. In family life infidelity and divorce fragment the basic cell of society. The scattering of the pieces often produces the mayhem of deliquent children and unstable adults. When a country is at odds within itself, the civil war that follows is universally acknowledged to be the most brutal war there is. When nations violate each other's rights the ultimate consequence is global catastrophe and mega-death.

Man's moral life is the microcosm where the drama of the principle is played out. When his heart is divided the evil takes root. It spreads its influence into every dimension of his existence. It even affects his natural environment. In Shakespeare's time it was thought to disrupt the very heavenly bodies in the harmony of their spheres.

The divided heart was the target of the Old Testament's greatest prophets. From the beginning it was regarded as the basic flaw that eventually unravels the whole. '"How long will you go limping with two different opinions?", challenged Elijah on Mount Carmel. '"If the Lord is God, follow him; but if Baal, then follow him". And the people did not answer him a word' (1 Kings 18:21). The failure to choose was a choice in itself against God. Not to acknowledge this was to prevent healing. As the children of Israel were about to enter the Promised Land, even as they stood on its borders, Moses' last charge to them was the same. 'See, I have set before you this day life and good, death and evil . . . Blessing and curse; therefore choose life . . . that you may dwell in the land' (Deut. 30:15; 19; 20). And again, before the twelve tribes under Joshua dispersed to claim their alloted inheritance, lest their dispersion should break their unity, the successor of Moses goaded them into decision. '"If you be unwilling to serve the Lord, choose this day whom you will serve . . . You cannot serve the Lord; for he is a holy God; he is a jealous God" . . . And the people said to Joshua, "Nay; but we will serve the Lord". Then Joshua said to the people, "You are witnesses against yourselves that you have chosen the Lord, to serve him . . . Then incline your heart to the Lord, the God of Israel"' (Josh. 24:15; 19; 21−22).

The only cure for the divided heart, source of every moral disunity throughout the universe, is the lanced heart of the Calvary Christ. Because it was indissolubly one − within itself, with all men including his enemies, and with the Father in the Holy Spirit − it was incapable of moral rupture even when touched by the sin of the world. So although it was dissected by the centurion's spear it suffered no division. Therefore it unleashed the inherent power of its own goodness and integrity which destroyed the evil that attacked it. Henceforth the hearts of men would be broken by repentance, rent by compassion at the sight of such great love. Addressing catechumens St John Chrysostom's spiritual interpretation of the cross set itself to deepen this conversion of the heart. 'The gospel relates that when Christ had died and was still hanging on the cross, the soldier approached him and pierced his side with the spear ... That soldier pierced his side: he breached the wall of the holy temple, and I found the treasure and acquired the wealth' (*Instructions to Catechumens*, 3).

The treasure that emerged from the side of the dead Christ was his bride, the Church. Like Adam asleep, from whose side the Lord God in Eden drew forth the rib that became his wife Eve, so Jesus provided flesh from his flesh, bone from his bone to give life to a spouse whom he would love as his own body. 'For no man ever hates his own flesh, but nourishes and cherishes it, as Christ does the Church ... This is a great mystery, and I mean in reference to Christ and the church' (Eph. 5:29; 32).

This union between Christ and the Church is the seed of the Kingdom on earth. It is the only antidote to evil. Through an indefectible marriage Christ draws into his wholesomeness all who come to him through the Church. All that is ruptured by sin is to be made complete again through the perfect espousal of priestly bridegroom and priestly bride, royal head and royal members, holy temple built on holy cornerstone. For this reason Christ's Church is called Catholic. It preserves within it the full means towards salvation with which Christ endowed it. For the same reason the Church is also called One. By its very nature it cannot be otherwise since Christ is one. Faith therefore professes it to be Holy. Despite the sin of its individual members it is in essence Christ's body, his spouse, and the Holy Spirit is its real life. Hence it is Apostolic, raised up from the very foundation stones whose witness is the cement of unity, the measure of truth, the basis of true faith. The four characteristics guarantee the quality of the seed. Each of them opposes its evil counterpart in the world: the un-Oneness or disintegration of community; un-Holiness or alienation from God; un-Catholicity, that is the fragmentation of truth; and un-Apostolicity which weakens the bond between the present time and the past historical event of salvation. Together, the marks of the Kingdom signal the end of disorder, the severing of its roots if not yet the blighting of its blossom.

And yet the visible Church still wrestles with the fungus of its un-nature. Bitterness still divides ecclesial traditions; sin has to be continually forgiven; its ministerial resources of word and sacrament are not fully received; pride and independence set some apart from the authentic witness of the apostolic teaching. How can this be in Christ's body, his bride, his temple?

The parables of the Kingdom in the synoptic gospels speak in images of growth. The seed itself is good seed, but the crop requires time. The Kingdom is like a field sown which sprouts up during the night, no farmer knows how. The Kingdom is like a mustard seed, smallest of all in the beginning but destined to shelter the birds of the air. The Kingdom is like wheat planted among darnel so that the two increase side by side until the harvest. The implication is clear. Life in God's reign on earth does not imply present perfection. But for those who remain his subjects — struggling at times but fundamentally faithful — the success of the seed is assured, like the certainty of faith itself. Through them the unity and peace of the cosmos is taking place invisibly as the underground root-system of a wheat-crop which in due season will reveal the fruits of the Kingdom.

Vatican 11 saw the Church's relationship with the world as a close, reciprocal one. Inter-penetration was the word it used. The gospel values influence the quality of life in society even as the Church conforms to the shape of that society age by age through its baptised members who are also citizens. At the same time the aims of Church and State are not congruous and must be differentiated. Thus 'earthly progress ought to be carefully distinguished from the growth of Christ's kingdom'. Nevertheless 'to the extent that the former can contribute to the better ordering of human society, it is of vital concern to the Kingdom of God' (GS, §39). By the same token the Church has much to offer the pursuit of earthly progress. 'Notably in the way it heals and elevates the dignity of the human person, in the way it consolidates society, and endows the daily activity of men with a deeper sense and meaning' (GS, §40).

In the universal struggle against evil which is common to all who espouse progress, and particularly progress in world peace, this emphasis on human dignity is what unites every effort for good. Here the desire of the nations converges on the aim of the Kingdom. But because the nations rely on earthly means for achieving what they desire, and because the citizens of the Kingdom on earth are still vulnerable to sin, respect for the human person is not always recognized as the cornerstone of positive growth. Vatican 11 acknowledges this and urges mankind to perceive here the radical symptom of the world's disorder. 'Peace cannot be obtained on earth unless the welfare of man is safeguarded ... A firm determination to respect the dignity of other men and other peoples along with the deliberate practice of fraternal love are absolutely necessary for the achievement of peace. Accordingly, peace is also the fruit of love, for love goes beyond what justice can ensure' (GS, §78).

Only sacrifice can bring about what the Kingdom promises. Only the incarnation of Christ can persuade that such sacrifice is worthwhile. In his birth as man, by his death for others, Jesus reveals the hidden glory of human nature in each person — no matter how depraved — and the worthiness of each person in God's eyes of love. This is why every other ideology, even humanism, falls short of what is needed; why 'peace must be built up continually ... (with) constant effort ... and unceasing vigilance' (GS, §78). The kind of love that forms real communion, true fellowship, lasting peace, and that defeats the power of evil is a supernatural gift, a divine quality which cannot be had by negotiation or acquired by mere effort of the will. It comes about rather by a humble acceptance of the royal Christ and obedience to his Spirit. 'For after we have obeyed the Lord, and in his Spirit nurtured on earth the values of human dignity, brotherhood and freedom, and indeed all the good fruits of our nature and enterprise, we will find them again, but freed of stain, burnished and transfigured. This will be so when Christ hands over to the Father a kingdom eternal and universal: "a kingdom of truth and life, of holiness and grace, of justice, love and peace". On this earth that kingdom is already present in mystery. When the Lord returns, it will be brought into full flower' (GS, §40).

Until he returns, while the Advent of time continues, the Church will not cease to pray for that Kingdom to come in which all the desires of the human heart will be satisfied and men of clay will live in peace.

Chapter Eight

O Emmanuel

December 23rd. O Emmanuel, you are our king and judge, the One whom the peoples await and their Saviour. O come and save us, Lord, our God.

The last of the seven titles of Jesus before the Vigil of Christmastide is without doubt the most beautiful of all. Emmanuel: God-with-us. Both in the sound of the word and its meaning, the Christian mystery is summed up succinctly and mellifluently. In Jesus, God is personally present to the world. On the eve of the Nativity 'Emmanuel' is telling those who wait for God that he is closer than they could possibly imagine. In that name God and man are hyphenated, conjoined forever, just as God's nature and ours are conjoined in the one to whom the name belongs. God, through his Son, with us in Jesus the man. The marvellous depth of the incarnation is given here for our contemplation in a single word. As long as our capacity for wonder lasts, the wonder of this miracle will never be exhausted. In two of his Christmas sermons, Pope St Leo the Great touched on its perennial freshness.

O Christian, be aware of your nobility − it is God's own nature that you share (Sermon 1, On the Nativity) ... O man, rouse yourself! Learn to know the dignity of your nature ... When our Lord Jesus Christ, whilst never ceasing to be true God, was born true man, he himself became the prelude of a new creation, and in the manner of his coming he gave the human race a spiritual beginning. What mind can understand this mystery, what

112

tongue can do justice to this gift of grace? (Sermon 7, On the Nativity).

It was to underline the mystery and acknowledge the grace that the writer of Matthew's Infancy Narrative carefully translated the ancient prophecy of Isaiah for his Jewish-Christian audience. 'All this took place to fulfil what the Lord had spoken by the prophet: "Behold, a virgin shall conceive and bear a son, and his name shall be called Emmanuel (which means, God with us)" (1:22–23). This same Gospel closes with an echo of that name, a reverberation of its enduring relevance for the post-ascension community about to face its unknown future. 'And Jesus came and said to them, . . . "lo, I am with you always, to the close of the age"' (28:20). As he had been God-with-them from the beginning, so he would always be Emmanuel for them through his most intimate self-revelation in the Spirit. As Spirit and Truth he would continue to dwell – glorified – in the midst of his Church, its strength and guiding principle through salvation history.

God's immanence was never a mere feature of that history. His presence *is* salvation. The fact became apparent in Old Testament times when, in the form of Father, God first revealed his existence as Creator and Liberator. His work prepared men for his fuller presence in the New Testament as Jesus, Redeemer and Mediator. In this final age of the plan, the age of the Church, he is internally present as Spirit: the Sanctifier and Giver of Life. Just as the Father revealed the Son to the world, and through the Son the Paraclete, so in the Paraclete mankind is united with the Son through whom we are brought to the Father. In the perfect symmetry of this 'figure of eight' is the shape of salvation. It defines a commitment that is fully Trinitarian, God's total presence in time to us as First, Second and Third Persons.

The significance of this point cannot be over-estimated. It explains the covenants, promises and deliverances of the Old Dispensation; the teachings, miracles, the sufferings of the New; and the charisms, sacraments and ministries of the time since. Through each phase of the story, by means of the features appropriate to each, the Divine comes close to us as power for good. A creative, redeeming and sanctifying

power that initiates, supports and completes the grace of salvation in the face of those evil forces that St Paul spoke of,
which have constantly threatened the spiritual destruction of
mankind from the beginning.

Throughout scripture, the effect of God's presence is
portrayed as an enabling grace for those called to assist his
plan in its practical unfolding. Moses, for example, insecure
and fretful as always in the execution of his task, would not
leave Horeb on the last leg of the exodus without the personal assurance of God's companionship. 'Moses said to the
Lord, "If your presence will not go with me, do not carry us
up from here. For how shall it be known that I have found
favour in your sight, I and your people? Is it not in your
going with us, so that we are distintct, I and your people,
from all other people that are on the face of the earth?" ...
And the Lord said, "My presence will go with you, and I
will give you rest"' (Exod. 33:15–16, 14). When the reins
of office are handed over to his successor, Joshua is thrice
promised the same sacred resource. 'As I was with Moses,
so I will be with you; I will not fail you or forsake you'
(Josh. 1:5; 9; 17). Therefore he must 'be strong and of
good courage!' – the admonition is repeated four times in
that same chapter to show that in God's closeness to men is
man's fitness for the work of God.

The same ideas re-occur, linked, in the Psalms of David.
This time it is in celebration of the King's victory over his
enemies, a victory which is also YHWH's.

> O Lord, your strength gives joy to the King,
> How your saving help makes him glad.
> You have made him rejoice with the joy of your presence
> (Ps.20/21).

Two things cause the King's joy: the Lord's strength, the
Lord's presence. They are therefore the same thing: God's
closeness is the King's strength, his chief asset in war. The
battle successes of David, like the Exodus and the Settlement
– all of them turning points in the fortunes of the Chosen
People – are hinges which require and receive the lubri-
cation of God himself. Like a holy oil of anointing his
presence facilitates progress from one stage to the next. The

more difficult the challenge for men, the more impressive the achievement of God.

No one understood the truth of this more than the prophets. Especially the young Jeremiah who learned the lesson early in his prophetic career when the Lord waved aside his feeble protestations on the grounds of immaturity. 'Do not say, "I am only a youth"; for to all to whom I send you you shall go . . . Be not afraid of them, for I am with you, says the Lord' (Jer. 1:7–8). Later he was to pass on the fruits of his experience to the nation in its hour of need. Writing to the Hebrew exiles in Babylon, he offered a sure consolation: 'For thus says the Lord: When seventy years are completed, I will visit you . . . and bring you back . . . I will be found by you . . . and I will restore your fortunes' (29:10–14). An impossible promise in the circumstances! Yet Jeremiah knew the power of the Lord's accompanying presence, of his visitation, and the effect that could have on a disheartened, enfeebled people.

This was the very power that Isaiah offered Ahaz on the occasion of the Immanuel prophecy: God's immanence at a time of impending calamity. Even though great hardship was afoot, they would survive the ordeal with vigour. Like the birth of a child to a maiden which guarantees a future even to the elderly who, though they themselves must die, know that their seed lives on. This young woman of Isaiah's time – was she perhaps giving birth to Ahaz's son? – would call her child 'God-with-us', to show her own firm belief in her country's future. Where God is present, there hope dwells too, another tomorrow is assured, is born and will grow. Isaiah points to the young woman and her child in the womb and its special name and her quiet hope in that birth. Prophet and prophetess, each of them touched a vein of truth that outlived its own time and context. It is this truth and the hope it brings that the Church celebrates at Christmas in the 'Emmanuel' title. In Jesus born of Mary, the enabling grace of God's saving presence takes on physical shape in the historical person of God's Son. From the virginal womb that is pure faith, that is all hope, that stands for a people who perceive deliverance entirely in terms of God's coming, is born God's personal response – his very Self. 'O Emmanuel . . . whom the peoples await and their Saviour, O come and save us, Lord, our God'.

There is a second sense in which Emmanuel is God with us. Not only as enabling grace but as divine solidarity. With us, as opposed to against us. Morally supportive of all that we do as human beings. In the sense that Jesus himself often meant when he said that 'He who is not against you is for you' (Luke 9:50; 11:23; Mark 9:40; Matt. 12:30). Nothing debilitates more than the feeling that everything is loaded against you, that no one supports you. Mere presence, whether physical or spiritual, is not enough to lift that weight. What is needed is the force of another's commitment to back you, the sense that there is someone 'rooting' for you, one who is on your side, pleading your cause, taking your part. Christ is that kind of strength for his people.

St Paul experienced this first hand when he arrived at Corinth. There was much organized opposition to his work there. He was openly reviled by the leading Jews of the city who even tried to prosecute him in the civil law courts. Prior to this his message had been ridiculed at Athens. They had laughed him out of the Areopagus. Extremely humiliated, he left Athens and never returned. Now he faced a similar misfortune in Achaia. But 'the Lord said to Paul one night in a vision, "Do not be afraid, but speak and do not be silent; for I am with you, and no man shall attack you to harm you"' (Acts 18:9–10).

It was all that Paul required. Within eighteen months he established by his preaching a community that was exemplary among the Christian cells of Greece. Corinth shone like a pearl because of its charisms, ministries, enthusiasm and organization. What the apostle achieved, what he taught this community to expect, was that '(God's) grace is sufficient' (2 Cor. 12:9), that is, the moral support that his closeness brings to the downhearted.

Discouragement is arguably the greatest danger within the Church today. The fear that one is swimming against an impossible tide. Or that the boat is sinking and that one will inevitably have to jump like so many others. The disheartening thought that one's efforts are in vain since, with the fall-off in religious practice and the decline in moral standards, one works alone. It was probably Jesus' intensest pain; it lasted through his entire passion. In his agony at Gethsemane he chided Simon Peter, 'So, could you not watch with me one hour?' (Matt. 26:40), and to James and John as well, 'My soul is very sorrowful, even to death; remain here, and watch with me' (Matt. 26:38). He who is called Emmanuel knew very well how bitter it is to lack support; what comfort there would be in fellowship, understanding, some sympathy, moral solidarity. In his humanity God experienced what in his divinity he had never needed: the importance of having someone to stand by you when you undertake the salvation of the world. It is this that makes his Christmas title so moving for those who reflect on it, so meaningful to those who feel they stand alone.

The epitome of the divine compassion expressed in the Emmanuel lies in the dual direction of its meaning. Not only is God with us, but in Jesus he desires that we should also be with him. 'Father, I desire that they also . . . may be with me where I am' (John 17:24). Henceforth the disciples would identify themselves in community in these terms. Where two or three are gathered in his name, there he would be in their midst (Matt. 18:20). That closeness to him was in fact the first mark of their calling. 'He went up into the hills, and called to him those whom he desired; and they came to him. And he appointed twelve, to be with him . . .' (Mark 3:13–14). Soon this companionship with the Lord came to be the distinguishing sign by which others recognized them. 'This man was with Jesus of Nazareth', the maid accused Peter on the night of the arrest. 'You were with Jesus the Galilean' (Matt. 26:71; 69. Cf. Mark 14:67; Luke 22:56). And when Judas Iscariot's death left a vacancy among the Twelve, this was one of the criteria that decided who was eligible for candidacy: '(Judas) was numbered among us . . . So (now) one of the men who have accompanied us during all the time that the Lord Jesus went in and out among us . . . – one of these men must become with us a witness to his resurrection' (Acts 1:17, 21–22).

This communion with Christ is the effect of his communion with us. It is the antidote to discouragement and despair. Positively, it is the substance of what it means to be the Church. The Church is a communion in Christ and with

Christ. As such the moral support it embodies is two-fold. Not just the psychological sense of well-being that is in fact so important on the human level. But more: the spiritual-moral support by which sin is overcome or forgiven — what we normally term grace. The two dimensions are not separate however. Through the course of the gospels their interaction is made plain and emphasized. The healing of the leper for example is accomplished by his encounter with Christ. It is completed, though, by his re-integration into the community of the living from which his disease — symbol of sin — had excommunicated him. Ironically it was Jesus who, by the end of the story, 'could no longer openly enter a town, but was out in the country' (Mark 1:45). In other words he had exchanged places with the diseased man, accepting his isolation so that the leper might be re-integrated into the fold of the healthy. One is not wrong to read the incident as a parable of the cross, whereby Jesus Emmanuel took upon himself men's isolation from God in order to reinstate his creatures in harmony with the Father. Bestowing on sinners that fellowship which is the inner nature of the Triune God, the Son tolerated in his human nature the sense of alienation which was anathema to him as Son — 'My God, my God, why have you forsaken me?' (Matt. 27:46) — thereby proving by his suffering the extent to which his name, 'With-us', was true.

The implications of this are significant in many areas. They cause us to review our perception of the problem of pain for example. When one invokes Jesus as Emmanuel, one cannot logically accuse God of indifference to human suffering, particularly that of the innocent. While the incarnation and cross do not explain affliction, they certainly place the discussion of it on a new level. We can no longer speak of the anomaly of evil in a good universe, or demand why children die under the eye of a just God, without also asking why the heavenly Father permitted, nay willed, the sacrifice of his own Child, Emmanuel.

What the Christmas name tells us in this matter is that God is closest to people when they are suffering. If the gospel does not account for suffering, suffering accounts for the gospel, the good news. It is not that pain is good, but that the goodness of God materializes through the pain of living and dying. Indeed it cannot be experienced except through suffering, which is itself then inexplicably trans-formed into a power for growth, for life. This *is* good news and has been accepted as such by Christians for two thousand years. The only unbearable pain would be to suffer alone without a source of compassion, or to suffer point-lessly, to no good purpose, without some benefit being derived from it. For those who celebrate Christmas, the unbearable is removed by the person of Emmanuel whose death gives meaning to all that his members endure for the sake of redemption, and whose presence in pain is the highest form of compassion.

This is why euthanasia for instance is simply not on the agenda in a Christian society. To consider this as a viable response to human suffering is to deny utterly the mystery of Christ and of Christianity. God's historical manifestation of himself in our midst, with us, was precisely to dignify all aspects of our common humanity, including those which St Paul says we introduced into the scenario by our sin, that is our frailty, mortality, vulnerability. Christian tradition teaches us to discover salvation through these things, not apart from them. The incarnation showed us how. At that moment God, anointed with human frailty, himself anointed pain with a kind of sacramental significance, giving it power to sanctify and make divine.

The third mode in which God is present is linked to the other two. If in the Father he is with us as an enabling presence, and in the Son as compassionate fellow man, he is also in our midst as Paraclete. The word can be translated as Advocate or Counsellor, or even Protector. It literally means One who is called to our side. John's Gospel also refers to him as Holy Spirit and the Spirit of Truth. Jesus described him as 'another' Paraclete, signifying that he shared the personal characteristics attributed to Jesus himself. Those characteristics define his role in relation to us, as do his various titles. They describe the manner in which God is with us as Spirit, a manner that supercedes the physical and goes beyond even the moral dimension, fulfilling both by bringing about the purpose of each. That purpose is the same as the purpose of the entire scheme of salvation: to complete the intimacy between God and man that was intended from the start but was then interrupted by sin. The first stage of that process was the revelation of God in himself. The second, the revelation of God-with-us in Jesus. The third stage accomplished by the Spirit is, as St Paul pointed out to the Colossians, 'Christ *in you*, the hope of glory' (Col. 1:27), the establishment in mystery of that communion whereby we become, even now, the dwelling-place of God on earth.

As Protector he is called by the Church to its side to safeguard this communion. He does so by witnessing to the truth. Convicting the world of sin, he distinguishes between the world and Jesus' disciples, not removing them from the world but keeping 'them from the evil one' (John 17:15) just as Jesus prayed he might. The Evil One, against whom the Spirit of Truth protects, is Satan, father of lies. 'Satan' means 'The Accuser'. Scripture depicts him as constantly accusing God's faithful people both in the Old and New Testaments. The Paraclete is a sure defender against his machinations: the distortion, confusion, fear, discouragement and loss of faith to which the Church is constantly subjected. By his truth, drawn from 'whatever he hears' from the Father and the Son (John 17:13), the Spirit calls to mind all that Jesus taught, declares things yet to come, reveals much that Jesus was not able to impart to his friends before his death, and guides them into all truth. In these ways he guards with his truthfulness all that Christ won to himself for God and which Christ, despite his absence from among us, in no way loses because of his continuing presence within us. For, as he promised, his Spirit not only 'dwells with you', but 'will be in you' (John 14:17) as Counsellor and Protector and Advocate.

Apart from love, there is no greater experience of personal presence – whether human or divine – than in truth. No greater sense of communion. Which explains why it is on this level that the Accuser, Satan – also known as the Adversary – launches the attack. Why too the Spirit of God, the Advocate or Defender, is needed to complete the work of the Son and of the Father. Even in the Old Testament there seems to have been an implicit consciousness of this. The Susanna story is a case in point. The upright woman, true daughter of Israel, stands wrongly accused of adultery. She is about to be condemned and executed for there is no one to defend her or take her part. She makes an emotive appeal to the 'eternal God who discerns what is secret ... and who knows that these men have borne false witness' (Dan. 13:42–43). Suddenly, even as she is being led away, a youth in the crowd steps forward. 'The Lord heard her cry ... God aroused the holy spirit of a young lad named Daniel; and he cried out with a loud voice, "I am innocent of the blood of this woman"'(13:44–46). Not *the* Holy Spirit, but a holy spirit. Not God himself, but Daniel. And yet God is the actor, the influence, the Prime Mover, because he is the ultimate truth to which he himself bears witness. The story concludes with the applause of the congregation in an outburst of prayerful adoration: 'Then all the assembly shouted loudly and blessed God, who saves those who hope in him' (13:60). The nearness of the God who defends the just, vindicates the virtuous, justifies the upright, impressed itself on this assembly, foreshadowing the Church's Christmas awareness of the God-within who pleads our cause at all times; of the God who, as St Paul observes, 'helps us in our weakness ... the Spirit (who) intercedes for us with sighs too deep for words' (Rom. 8:26).

But our concept as Christians of the Advocacy of God goes much further than the Jewish notion portrayed in the Susanna narrative. She after all was an innocent victim. In the companion story that accompanies this reading in the liturgy, that of John Chapter 8, the woman is in fact an adulteress. She personifies the sinful humanity of the Church's members. And yet she was equally justified by the word of the Word made flesh, by the Spirit of his mouth, by the breath of his lips. 'Jesus looked up and said to her, "Woman, has no one condemned you?" She said "No one, Lord". And Jesus said, "Neither do I condemn you; go, and do not sin again"' (vv.10–11). Even though this passage is not Johannine, it perfectly illustrates the spirit and intention of John's Gospel. 'For God sent his Son into the world, not to condemn the world, but that the world might be saved through him' (John 3:17). What makes the Fourth Gospel different from the others is the way it stresses the Holy Spirit's role in achieving God's intent. If Jesus is the 'one Mediator' of the Pastoral Epistles, his Spirit is the 'other Advocate' of the Johannine corpus. That is, it is by the power and presence of the third Person, Christ's best gift to the world, that the fruit of Christ — the Father's best gift — is gathered in like a good harvest. The Holy Spirit's mediatorship, his advocacy on behalf of the sinful as well as the just, is in itself the epitome of God's immanence in every sense of that word. Just how remarkable is this faithfulness of the Christian God, Paul himself underlines in his famous exclamation, 'The love of God has been poured into our hearts by the Holy Spirit which has been given to us ... What proves that God loves us is that Christ died for us while we were still sinners' (Rom. 5:5; 8). The two phases of the plan are intrinsically linked: what Christ accomplished in the flesh has been realized and completed in the Spirit. In so doing the Paraclete completes also the meaning of Emmanuel, rounding it to the fullness of that figure of eight which we spoke of earlier, so that in us and with us and through us God is becoming all in all.

While we are aware of the Trinitarian dimensions of God's presence with us as the believing and praying community of God's making, yet it is to Christ alone that we address the Emmanuel of the 'O' antiphon on December 23rd. Not to the Father or the Spirit. We do so in imitation of Holy Scripture wherein this is a distinctly christological title; in imitation also of Sacred Tradition, that is the liturgical tradition which precedes theological reflection, out of which the formulated doctrine emerges. That same liturgy directs every act of worship to the Father via Christ, and never otherwise. 'Through him, with him and in him' all glory and honour in the unity of the Spirit are channelled towards the Godhead (from the 'Doxology'). Jesus is at the centre of the figure of eight. There is no passage out from God nor back again to him without the Son. No knowledge of the Father, no life in the Spirit apart from Christ. No communion with the divine, no transformation of humanity, no liberation from sin, no hope of heaven, no fulfilment of scripture, nor of the promises nor covenants without him. No God-with-us. No Emmanuel without Mary's child. Hence the extraordinary rejoicing which his very name inspires, and which his birth invites.

The title therefore affirms the entire heart of the Christian faith: that there is no salvation outside or apart from Jesus of Nazareth, born at Bethlehem, crucified on Calvary, raised at Easter and glorified at the right hand of the Father. Putting the matter positively, the antiphon affirms with confidence that all who are saved − all the so-called 'anonymous Christians', all those who seek God in good faith but do not yet know him, all who serve him in ignorance by following their conscience − are somehow 'in Christ'. Although this has to be in a manner unknown to us, it is nonetheless so. It is therefore another reason for praising God and rendering homage at the manger with the wise. With them we recognize and acknowledge the call to the nations to come and adore. Christ is the centre of the universe, of history, and of the human race. This centre is also the centre of God's redemptive plan. The concentric point where all things meet and are reconciled and made one: the human and divine, earth and heaven, God and man.

It is not surprising that 'Emmanuel' should be the final acclamation expressed by the Church as Advent draws to a close and gives way to the One awaited. The Bible does the same. As Scripture anticipates the closing of the ages and presents its apocalyptic foretaste of heaven, it is the God-with-us that emerges as the final image. In a strange mixture of present and future tenses the vision is still a hope to be realized as well as a promise fulfilled. 'Behold, the dwelling of God is with men. He will dwell with them, and they shall be his people, and God himself will be with them' (Rev. 21:3). The central character is Christ the Lamb. By his blood and by the testimony of the Lamb's followers the Accuser is thrown down, defeated, cast out (12:7−11). It is Michael who captains the victory. Michael − his name means One who is like God (like Jesus himself, God's perfect image) − was the traditional defender of the remnant of Israel. His military prowess against the power of Darkness dramatizes the spiritual power of the Lamb who, by his incarnation, is the real defender of the people. By his sacrifice, shared with the martyrs and all who have undergone death-to-self, he is the Proto-Paraclete, the source of salvation. He is so in union with the Father and the Spirit on the one hand, and in union with his people the Church on the other. As Victor, as Saviour, as Lamb, he is Emmanuel. As Emmanuel he brings with him his Father and their Spirit. ('If anyone loves me, he will keep my word, and my Father will love him, and we will come to him and make our home with him ... and the Father will send in my name, the Holy Spirit' [John 14:23; 26]). That promise and its projected fulfilment brings the revelation of the Word to an end, just as the seventh title brings Advent to its end.

This end however is nothing other than a new beginning. What has gone before is but a preparation, a time of conversion, a time for listening, for desiring. The Church, like Mary, knows that its expectancy will soon give way to Nativity. Like the writer of the Apocalypse, like the Maiden giving birth, the community hears in faith an answer to its acclamations, its supplication, its antiphons. In the heart of prayer it senses the ultimate promise of Emmanuel − 'Surely I am coming soon' − and echoes the response of the Visionary who speaks on behalf of all: 'Amen, Come, Lord Jesus!'(Rev. 22:20)

Chapter Nine

This Hallowed Time

When we look over the christological titles of Advent, what we see is a range of sacred similes. Christ is not in fact the rising sun, but he is like it. He is not a key, he is not a root, but something of what they are he is. Like all the metaphorical devices of the scriptures as literature, they throw light on the incomprehensible. Jesus was no lamb, no lion of Judah, no vine, no loaf, no shepherd, and yet he was all of these and more by analogy. Similarly with the antiphons. As Wisdom he is known to us through his teaching. As Adonai his personal identity is revealed as God. He is Root of Jesse insofar as God has assumed our human nature, inherited a genealogy. The Key of David explains why he became man: to unlock the gates of salvation. The Morning Star, the Rising Sun, tells us how. He is the Desire of Nations inasmuch as his victory is the principle of unity and peace. He is for us Emmanuel because, as God-with-us, his achievement of redemption is forever.

Placed together these similes form a kind of identikit picture of the One whom we expect. They blend different aspects of the Messiah whose features the Advent Church, like the woman in pregnancy, tries to imagine and identify. The time-honoured images of Advent are ways of approaching him who is unknowable. They are like the contours on the face of the incarnate Son of God whose human features make visible the invisible love of the Godhead. We have adapted them from our experience – from the cycle of the seasons, the history of religious sensibility, from the culture of Scripture and Tradition. In all this we touch the incarnational aspect of our faith, the need to put concrete form on that which transcends our present existence. Thus we learn to incorporate all that we feel, sense, touch, hear and see, into our search for God.

Sacred similes deepen not only our knowledge of God but also our desire for him. St Augustine saw this as the purpose of prayer: '(God) wants our desire to be exercised in prayer, thus enabling us to grasp what he is preparing to give ... We shall have the capacity to receive it ... the more ardently we desire ... Thus the apostle's saying, "Pray without ceasing", means nothing else but: without ceasing, desire, from him who alone can give it, the blessed life, which is none other than eternal life' (Ep. 130, To Proba). Drawing upon our experience of life and reflecting on that, we intone the antiphonic titles to increase our longing for the mystery of Christ. As with faith, it is only to those who desire that understanding is given. The antiphons are therefore the expression of a reflective, faith-filled desire for deeper communion with the new-born Lord through a mature appreciation of his identity and mission. They are also the means by which that desire is satisfied, for in the very process of intoning them, repeating them, contemplating them, the prayer is answered. Through the consecration of the time in prayerful waiting, the time itself is fulfilled, is brought to its completion. Christ is born in spirit in the hearts of all who long for him. Thus it is a hallowed time, made holy by the union of God and Church in their common desiring.

The mystery of Christ that engages our search is not meant to leave us mystified. It is the Paschal Mystery. It enlightens the mind and reveals God to us. It opens to us the deep and mystic experience of Christ's life, death, resurrection and glorification. It is what Paul called the demonstration of the Spirit, with power to change our lives and attitudes, our perception of reality, our relationships with other people, ourselves, the entire universe, and with God himself. Each title illuminates the central mystery of salvation, highlights its graced colouring like the stained-glass windows of a rotund church which catch the rays of the sun as it passes on its diurnal course. Hence our pre-Christmas meditations in the last week before Nativity focus and re-focus our attention upon the ministry of Jesus, his intense suffering, his Easter appearances, his ascension and Pentecost.

Two questions immediately suggest themselves from this. One, is this not a poor method of mental prayer, tiringly repetitive, a thematic tautology? And two, isn't the Paschal theme more than a little out of place liturgically at Christmastide?

With regard to the first, it is true that we cover the same ground again and again in these meditations. However the pattern is not cyclic but spiral, and that makes a great difference. A circle suggests returning to the point from which one began with little progress. A spiral on the other hand implies that, while the same points of the compass are passed, the journey is always towards a new destination because it is a journey inwards. In to the heart of the matter, in to the centre of the vortex and, in the case of the Christian mystery, upwards to the higher levels of awareness of God. The hallowed time of Advent evokes the image of a cone. It is a model for conversion, for the change of heart that the prayer of the season requires of all who take prayer seriously. It also preserves the idea of continuity. The deposit of faith which energizes the spiral remains the same: complete in itself yet subject to development. The content of Christian faith can never be added to nor subtracted from, yet it does admit a continuing interpretation for greater understanding doctrinally and liturgically – the twin streams of spiritual nourishment. The vastness of the mystery surely accounts in part for why this final age of the Spirit has lasted so long, why the Parousia has been delayed – more so indeed than the first Christians could have imagined. Time is required to explore the dimensions of what God has revealed in Christ. Considering the millennia allowed to the Church for this, the spiralling cone is, finally, a model of hope. It implies that in God's scheme of things it is never too late to repent, to change, to move forward, to grow, to understand, to become wise.

The spiralling course of Advent's hallowed time stands at the crossroads of the two ancient concepts of history. The first, the Greek, saw life as a spinning wheel of fortune. Man is trapped on that wheel, sometimes racked upon its spokes. From age to age he profits little from his mistakes, repeating the same ones over and again. Powerless to halt its movement, unable to throw himself off, he is the victim of his own little tragedy, caught in the cruel sport of the gods. We have inherited something of this view in modern culture.

The other paradigm of history, typical of Hebrew thought, is that of the straight road with a beginning, a middle, and an end. According to this pattern we do not travel the same road twice, may not retrace our steps; we pass this way but once, each day dawns as a new experience. This concept has also entered into our modern consciousness. It stands with the other, sometimes predominating in our view of things, sometimes not.

Each classical vision has its drawbacks. The Greek, because it is so pessimistic; the Jewish, because it is so final about experience. Although both contain elements of truth neither tells the whole story. They tend to limit the possibilities of human beings as creatures-in-relation. They also fail to allow for the fact that Christ is Lord of history, that by his becoming flesh he entered into time, broke through its limitations, diffused his presence throughout all ages, redeeming the temporal dimension of creation as well as the spatial. His coming therefore is never restricted to a single epoch. His forgiveness transforms time past. His grace transfigures time present. His promise transignifies the future. In every phase of his coming it is through human relationships that he carries out his saving work, exercises his Lordship of love. This is why Advent really stands for all time, and why all time is hallowed, an opportunity for grace.

With regard to the second question – 'are not the titles more fitting to a Lenten or Easter meditation than a Christmas one' – the answer is already partly in place. No season is unsuited to reflection on the Paschal Mystery. Nativity is in service of Holy Week and Easter-tide. Christ was born to suffer and to die. His birth is the prelude to his death, just as his crucifixion is the prelude to his glorification. The mystery we are dealing with is not fragmented. It is one. The fact that the secular celebration of Christmas is often devoid of any reference to Good Friday or the resurrection is perhaps why people frequently complain about the over-commercialization of the Christian feast. Are they not (rightly) reacting to the anomaly of a world that contradicts the holy purpose of the festivities by gross indifference to the spiritual values it announces? Once the shadow of the cross is excluded from the illumination of the crib, such indifference is actually inevitable.

The 'O' antiphons are intended to redress this anomaly. By directing attention to the whole Christ, the full span of his incarnation, they bring mankind back to the basics of the Christian religion. They remind us that the mystery of Christ is to be accepted wholly. We dare not retain only those aspects that we find attractive while rejecting those we find unpalatable. To do so would be to follow 'another gospel' — what St Paul feared the Galatians had done (Gal. 1:6 – 9). The consequence of such a thing, the Apostle warned, is to be disinherited from the kingdom of God (Gal. 6:21).

When Paul used the term *musterion*, which is the focus of the pre-Christmas antiphons, he meant the plan of salvation conceived by the Father, carried out by the Son, and lived in the Spirit. That it may equally be translated 'mystery' fitted his understanding of the matter perfectly. Hidden from before the ages, this holy plan was fully unveiled in the appearance of God's Son on earth. Its purpose was to make of all men his children, chosen as such for holiness through forgiveness of sin by the blood of Christ on Calvary (Eph. 1:3 – 8). Paul's hymn of praise over this concludes: 'For (God) has made known to us in all wisdom and insight the mystery (*musterion*) of his will, according to his purpose which he set forth in Christ as a plan for the fullness of time' (1:9 – 10). What makes Paul rejoice is that the formerly concealed solution to mankind's most fundamental problem has been made known to the world through Jesus of Nazareth, Messiah long-awaited. It is in the same spirit of joyful recognition that the Church prefixes its songs of praise with the Messianic acclamations. As the faith behind the songs increases, as the understanding of it soars, there is no question of omitting any part of the good news. The plan is perfect in its entirety even though it requires maturity to accept in the living out of Christian life. Indeed it is in acknowledgement of the difficulty of embracing the gospel in full that the praying, singing community meditates repeatedly on the same elements of the plan, the mysteries of Jesus' life and death. It is almost as if it were learning a demanding score that needed much practice to get right, but was worthy of a good performance.

Like good music too the mystery of Christ, though known, in a sense remains hidden. The musician, scanning the staff notation, knows roughly how the piece will sound, but not until it is fully presented by an orchestra will he be able to enjoy the accomplishment of the composition. By the same token the *musterion* of God's plan, while articulated in the Paschal Mystery and passed down through the proclamation of Word and Sacraments (the old term for which was the 'Mysteries'), still awaits its Grand Performance at the end of time. Because redemption depends on faith, that final sounding must remain obscure to us. If it were not, if the content of faith were clear beyond dispute, then belief would no longer be what it is, would no longer indeed be needed. It would have given way to perception; reason would demand our acquiescence; there would be no merit in accepting the truth on God's word alone, no freedom to make a personal response, and therefore no salvation.

At the same time faith is not without reason, is in no way unreasonable. The antiphons give us reasons in plenty for believing, because the truth they point to matches our experience of truth elsewhere: in the arts, the sciences, philosphy, and the wisdom of living. Moreover, in celebrating the meeting of the human and the divine in the incarnation, they affirm that the mystery is open to everyone. By drawing attention to the implications of the incarnation in terms of Jesus' Paschal ministry, they place the means to maturity and life within the reach of all. They do this not only through their content – the matter of Christ's life in the gospel; but also by the manner in which they present and proclaim that material. Earlier we suggested that the movement of Advent-time is spiral. The antiphons, their titles, acclamations, invocations and supplications are spiral in their movement too, but with a rhythm that carries the one who prays both in to the centre and out again. Like the rotating pendulum of a clock that traces circles to the right and to the left in even, gentle rings. Or like the steady, rhythmic breathing of one who has composed himself in contemplative self-awareness.

This movement in and out is a spiritual and theological

movement in three parts. The first, the movement towards the centre, is conversion: the process whereby one turns back again to God. The second phase is communion: the arrival-point where one encounters the stillness of the heart of God. The movement out again from this is mission, the third part of the experience. Here the beauty of God projects one back into the company of men so that others too can taste this stillness which we call salvation. This ultimately is the purpose of all liturgy: to convert, to unite, to commission. It is particularly the aim of the Advent liturgy as the seasonal preparation for Christmas. By the last week, when these three themes have been thoroughly explored through the readings at Mass and in the Office, each antiphon gathers up and encapsulates their essence (in the language of praise and intercession), and their spirit (in the rise and fall of its mantra-type structure).

This pattern which the antiphons embody so strikingly is the very pattern of the Mystery in the Scriptures and the Church's life. In Luke's Gospel for example it explains the movements of Mary. Even she, though sinless and full of grace, has to undergo the conversion experience. She does so by turning towards the word of God sent by the angel. Her acceptance of this word causes her to conceive the Word made flesh – the most significant moment of communion with God since the beginning of time. And from that mystical intimacy and physical bonding, she is immediately inspired to journey out to the house of Zechariah to greet Elizabeth and share with her the Spirit that she herself received: her mission.

It is the pattern also of the eucharistic celebration, life of the Church's life. Beginning with the Penitential Rite we ask forgiveness of God and each other. The Mystery we celebrate, which is that of the Covenant, cannot begin without this communitarian act of repentance. Phase one. It leads gently and naturally into an ever-deepening union with Christ through the Liturgy of the Word, the Liturgy of the Eucharist, and the Rite of Communion: the heart of the New Covenant. The Mass ends with the Dismissal: the blessing and commission to go out and bring this celebration to others in the sanctuary of the world through the liturgy of life and Christian love. Phase three.

The beauty of Advent is in the synthesis of these different forms of praying the Mystery: the Eucharist, the Scriptures, the 'O' Antiphons and the Hours. Through the four Sundays, and especially through the seven days before the Vigil of Nativity, one is caught up in the wonder of the gyrations of love. God and his Church dancing together in spirit, pirouetting in perfect synchrony down through the centuries and across the universe. All the forms come together in the Church's prayer as an expectant Church, celebrating what has already been revealed to it and through it, and confident therefore of what is yet to come.

*   *   *

It is now Christmas Eve, and we have come almost to the end of Advent. Soon it will be evening. The Vigil and the Feast are about to begin. The 'Short Response' at First Vespers reads: 'Today you know that the Lord will come. In the morning you will see his glory.' It strikes that note of confidence mentioned a moment ago. The very sequence of the antiphon titles reinforces the inner certainty. Taking in reverse the initial letters of their Latin originals − *E*mmanuel; *R*ex; *O*riens; *C*lavis; *R*adix; *A*donai; *S*apientia − we discover the acrostic, ERO CRAS: Tomorrow I will come! It is the Lord's hidden response to all who wait for him; to those who have called him in the last week of Advent; and to those who longed for him during the course of their Christian life. It is the echo of his ultimate promise at the end of the Apocalypse − 'Surely I am coming soon' (Rev. 22:20).

Soon a Child will be born for them. Soon a people will be born again too. 'In the morning you will see his glory.' The scriptural source of the 'Short Response' is the Book of Exodus. It was a reference to the manna from heaven promised by the Lord to the community of Israel in the desert. 'Moses and Aaron said to all the people, "At evening you shall know that it was the Lord who brought you out of the land of Egypt, and in the morning you shall see the glory of the Lord ... when the Lord gives you in the morning bread to the full"' (16:6−8).

That manna was the heavenly food with which God fed

his wandering tribes during their bitter pilgrimage in the wilderness. It sustained them for forty years until they entered the Land of Promise and partook of the fruits of their own sowing. This day God gives the flesh and blood of his Son to be the new manna. It comes from Bethlehem − House of Bread − located in the region called Ephrathah − meaning fertile. In the third century St Paula who, like Jerome, loved the place, articulated the mind and heart of the Church in every age when she wrote: 'O Bethlehem, I salute you, House of Bread where the Bread come down from Heaven saw the light of day. O Ephrathah, I hail you, field most rich and fertile among whose fruits has been numbered God himself.' We are reminded at the Midnight Eucharist by the Sacrament of his presence that all his promises are worthy of our belief, of our waiting; that in him all the titles of prophecy are fulfilled. Here every word is made complete in the Word made bread, all the wisdom of God's feeding lavishly distributed in the bread made flesh in those whose lives embody the word.

Christmas is especially the time of the Eucharist, the time of gentle Mary, the time of Emmanuel. It is the time of peace with God and each other, the time of grace. It is the dawn of a new day that heralds the eternal Day which will never set. Until that final fulfilment, this feast is above all a time when heaven breaks through to earth, and God's Kingdom − for however short a space − seems to hold sway over the forces of evil that hold the human heart in thrall for so much of the rest of the year. The idea is not a new one. No less than Shakespeare noted it as a tradition four centuries ago. Since it is from him that the title of this last chapter comes, we shall let him have the final word.

> Some say that ever 'gainst that season comes
> Wherein our Saviour's birth is celebrated,
> The bird of dawning singeth all night long:
> And then, they say, no spirit dare stir abroad,
> The nights are wholesome; then no planets strike,
> No fairy takes, nor witch hath power to charm,
> So hallow'd and so gracious is the time
> (*Hamlet*, 1, i, 158−164).